DIGITAL IMAGE PROCESSING

A PRACTICAL PRIMER

GREGORY A. BAXES

CASCADE
PRESS

P.O. Box 27613
Denver, Colorado 80227

Library of Congress Cataloging-in-Publication Data

```
Baxes, Gregory A.
  Digital image processing.

  Reprint. Originally published: Englewood Cliffs, N.J. :
Prentice-Hall, c1984.
  Bibliography: p.
  Includes index.
  1. Image processing--Digital techniques.  I. Title.
[TA1632.B38  1988]      621.36'7        87-73436
ISBN 0-945591-00-4 (pbk.)
```

This book originally published in 1984 by Prentice-Hall, Inc.

Printed in the United States of America.

1 2 3 4 5 6 7 8 9 10

ISBN 0-945591-00-4

Editorial/production supervision by Cyndy Lyle Rymer
Interior design by Maria Carella
Cover design by Jeannette Jacobs

*To Mom and Dad for their continual support
and Mr. Pitts, who first opened my eyes to the electronic world*

This book is available in all quantities by contacting —

**CASCADE
PRESS**

**P.O. Box 27613
Denver, CO 80227**

Contents

Preface

Digital image processing is a fascinating field that is just now beginning to reach into our everyday lives; It is no longer confined to the research environment. Stretching forward from its use almost exclusively in spacecraft imagery enhancement, digital image processing is finding exciting applications in automated factory control, robotics, security, and even hobby-level tinkering. It is emerging from what was once a mathematical engineering study to an applications-oriented field knowing few bounds.

Throughout the years, digital image processing has been supported by many publications, ranging from technical papers to textbooks. However, due to the mathematically complex subject matter, the thrust of interest has naturally remained somewhat theoretical. The individual without significant background in higher mathematics and electrical signal processing has found it difficult to fully grasp the complexities of the subject. It is the intent of this book to provide an elementary overview of digital image processing at a practical level. With this book acting as an initial building block, the interested reader may then more confidently proceed to the advanced texts when necessary.

The driver of an automobile does not need to master the workings of the internal combustion engine in order to drive the vehicle effectively. Similarly, a user need not understand all of the principles of digital image processing to apply certain techniques. Here, the reader is presented with the functional basics of digital image processing in a systematic manner that, most importantly, is illustrated through many pictorial graphics and photographs with a minimum of theory.

The mathematical proofs normally associated with the material herein have been reduced to a bare minimum. Instead, the reader wishing additional development of the topics is referred to the texts and papers listed in the further reading/references section, where the subjects are treated in a more mathematically rigorous manner.

The book is broken into four logical subsections, each serving a specific need and not all directed toward every reader's requirements. Part I, "Introduction to Image Processing," serves as an introduction to the field. The layman is brought into the image processing frame of reference—its definition, need, and applications. Digital image processing concepts are studied in Part II, "Processing Concepts." The idea of a digital image, the image histogram, and picture processing operations are covered in a format that brings to light the simplistic principles of digital image processing. Part III, "Processing Hardware," transfers the discussion into the hardware realm. Here, the block diagram level of discussion allows the reader to gain an insight into the hardware topics of image data handling and the image processor itself. An important section of the book is Part IV, "Processing in Action."

Part IV presents nineteen commonly used digital image processing operations in a guide format. Each Image Operation Study discusses an operation that is covered in Part II but with a more in-depth approach that contains, most importantly, several before-and-after photographs. The examples are detailed by the processing operation(s) implemented, mathematical and verbal description, process flow diagram, results, and applicable uses. It is through these "hands-on" demonstrations that the reader gains the biggest insight into the power of fundamental digital image processing operations. Reference is made to each Image Operation Study as coverage is encountered in the text of the book.

The scope of this book is broad, providing coverage on the introductory topics associated with digital image processing. Not all readers will find each section of equal interest. For instance, a person with some digital hardware background will discover Part III to be a valuable supplement to the adjoining material, whereas the individual seeking an overview of the subject and its capabilities will derive most satisfaction from Parts II and IV. In this respect, the book lends itself to a variety of reader levels and needs. Whether used in the lab as practical and visual support to a standard college-level text or as a primer for the uninitiated, this book is intended to provide a fundamental resource. Having read the book, the reader is armed with the foundation to implement and understand image processing at a workable level.

In acknowledgment, I wish to thank several individuals who helped make this book possible. All graphic figures were produced by Colette Piver, whose skill and artistic abilities in interpreting crude drawings are appreciated. The talents of Bert Kadzielawa aided immensely in the generation of the photographic material. Special thanks go to Debbie McAnally; without her many hours of typing and retyping, this manuscript would never have been completed.

INTRODUCTION TO IMAGE PROCESSING

What Is Image Processing? 1

The term *image processing* has become one of today's hottest key words in the applied computer sciences. What was once an expensive, time-consuming, and somewhat unpredictable endeavor has ripened into a mature discipline of its own. With the advent of inexpensive microprocessors, dense memory devices, and special purpose signal processing components, image processing has become a valuable tool in a variety of applications.

Image processing, in its general form, pertains to the alteration and analysis of pictorial information. We find instances of image processing occurring all the time in our daily lives. Perhaps the most common case is that of eyeglasses. Corrective eyeglasses serve to alter observed pictorial scenes in such a way that aberrations created by the eye are compensated for by correcting the image before its contact with the eye. Another common case of image processing is the adjustment of the brightness and contrast controls on a television set. By doing this, we enhance the image until its subjective appearance to us is most appealing. Even the water in a pond serves to alter the form of an image. The reflected image is not only reversed, but often exhibits distortion due to the water's motion. Probably the most powerful image processing system encountered in everyday life is the one comprised of the human eye and brain. This biological system receives, enhances, dissects, analyzes, and stores images at enormous rates of speed. Ironically, this system is taken more for granted than any other. All these are examples of image processing that are so commonly accepted that one rarely thinks of them as anything unique.

Methods of Image Processing

In the pursuit of image processing as a discipline, the objective is to visually enhance or statistically evaluate some aspect of an image not readily apparent in its original form. This objective is carried out through the development and implementation of the processing means necessary to operate upon images. Fundamentally, three techniques of implementing a process upon an image are available—one that is optical and two that are electronic, analog and digital. Although the analog and digital techniques are both electronic means, they differ considerably. Each of the three methods is found in routine use with the particular application defining the most practical approach to implementing the process in need.

Optical processing, as implied, uses an arrangement of optics to carry out a process. Eyeglasses are a form of optical image processing. An important form of optical processing is found in the photographic darkroom. For years, photographers have enhanced, manipulated, and abstracted images from one form to another, the object always being to produce a more favorable or appealing final print. This classical form of image processing has been refined through trial-and-error techniques, leaving today's photographer with a broad base of rules enabling quick and predictable results. The pioneers of the darkroom may probably be considered to be the first to use defined image processing techniques in their everyday work.

Analog processing of images refers to the alteration of images through electrical means. Of course, the image must be in an electrical form first. The most common example of this is the television image. The television signal is a voltage level that varies in amplitude to represent brightness throughout the image. By electrically altering this signal, we correspondingly alter the final displayed image appearance. The brightness and contrast controls on a television set serve to adjust the amplitude and reference of the video signal, resulting in the brightening, darkening, and alteration of the brightness range of the displayed image.

Digital image processing is a form of image processing brought on by the advent of the digital computer. Allowing the precise implementation of processes, this form provides the greatest flexibility and power for general image processing applications. Within the digital domain, an image is represented by discrete points of defined brightness. Each point has a numeric location within the image and a numeric brightness. By manipulating these values of brightness within the image, the computer is capable of carrying out the most complex operations with relative ease. Furthermore, the flexibility in the programming of a computer allows operations to be modified quickly, a feature that optical and analog processing inherently do not support.

The recent availability of sophisticated semiconductor digital devices and compact powerful computers, coupled with advances in image processing algorithms, has brought digital image processing to the forefront. Because of this, a new industry has been born. The prime products of this industry are computer hardware, software, and special peripherals developed to support the needs of digital image handling and processing. This intense activity has led to the development of digital image processing systems suitable in price and capability to be used in low-end applications previously denied the opportunity.

Digital Image Processing: A Historical Evolution

The roots of digital image processing may be traced back to the early 1960s. It was at this time that NASA was energetically pursuing its lunar science program in an attempt to characterize the lunar surface in support of the future Apollo program. The Ranger program was established, in part, to image the lunar surface, relaying the pictures to Earthbound scientists for evaluation. After several previous Ranger missions during which the video equipment failed to function, Ranger 7 transmitted several thousand images back to Earth. These television images were taken from their original analog electronic form and converted to a digital form. Subsequent digital processing of these image data was then carried out to remove various camera geometric and response distortions. It was this processing of Ranger 7 imagery that ushered the digital computer into the world of image processing.

This initial work in digital image processing was done at NASA's Jet Propulsion Laboratory in Pasadena, California. NASA then continued this funding of research and development in support of its other space programs. Following the Ranger program was a series of planetary exploration probes, all supported by digital image processing. The Mariner project returned images from the planets Mars, Venus, and Mercury. Project Surveyor soft-landed cameras on the lunar surface. Pioneer 10 and 11 spacecraft sent fly-by images of Jupiter and Saturn. The Viking spacecraft, equipped with cameras, landed on the surface of Mars. More recently, two Voyager spacecraft encountered the planets Jupiter and Saturn, and returned a wide range of imagery aiding in the scientific studies of these planets.

In addition to NASA's planetary imagery, various other government agencies such as the United States Geological Survey support various image processing activities.

Earth-orbiting satellites such as LANDSAT, TIROS, NIMBUS, GOES, and a variety of military surveillance systems return electronic Earth surface imagery on a day-to-day basis. Furthermore, their data are routinely processed at ground receiving stations through various digital computer systems prior to their use.

Good background on the origin and evolution of digital image processing is found in Further Reading/References I-3 and II-1.

Although the space program provided the initial impetus and funding for the research and development of image processing, the applications are not restricted to space imagery. Today, image processing is found in medical, factory automation, and robotics control applications. The ever-declining price and increasing availability of digital systems for image acquisition and handling has brought high-power processing capabilities to the user who once only dreamed of such possibilities. The microcomputer revolution has allowed the consumer to pursue various low-level computing activities. One such boom in the industry is in computer graphics. Graphics may be thought of as the synthetic generation of pictorial imagery. Of course, the next logical step is to provide real-life imaging capabilities. The computer is truly gaining the ability to see, making vision and image generation the next man-machine interface.

One such application of a low-level imagery project is that of the amateur radio satellite, OSCAR 9. This spacecraft, built by the University of Surrey, England, is to support a variety of scientific studies including Earth imaging. Once the satellite becomes operational, images are to be transmitted on standard amateur radio bands, allowing virtually anyone to receive them. With low-level image handling capabilities, the ham will be able to receive and display these images in the comfort of his or her own home. By the same token, simple image handling capabilities also allow images to be transmitted from one individual to another over standard telephone lines or on cassette tapes. These endeavors, combined with industry support, bring digital image processing to the level where average individuals may pursue it.

In the following pages, the field of digital image data handling and processing is introduced in a manner comprehensible to the interested individual. Image processing is introduced, overviewing common techniques and implementations. Additionally, the basic electronic hardware is discussed, giving a block-level idea of the methods employed in handling and processing image data. The attempt made here is to supply a practical introduction and reference to the field of digital image processing.

Digital Image Processing: The Basics 2

In this chapter, we explore the fundamental elements of digital image processing. First, the field of image processing is discussed in an operational context, where the various reasons for using these techniques are laid out. Following this, the processes for carrying out these operations are defined. Finally, the hardware system for implementing the processes is overviewed. The purpose of this chapter is to briefly introduce these subjects and serve as a foundation for their use throughout this book.

Image processing is a field that encompasses a broad range of capabilities. Any action that operates upon or uses pictorial information falls within the discipline of image processing. Two terms that will help in the comprehension of the field must be defined. An *image operation* is any action upon an image that is defined from an application's standpoint. When we speak of a particular operation, we are explaining what the desired result is to be. An *image process,* on the other hand, defines how a given operation is to be implemented. A process is a means of carrying out an operation. These are two distinctly separate concepts, analogous in many ways to the differences between computer software and hardware. We may now discuss image processing from both the operational and processing viewpoint.

Operational Breakdown

Three classes of image operations may be used to suitably subdivide the field into manageable parts (see Figure 2-1). They are: (1) *image quality enhancement*—operations that subjectively or objectively modify the appearance, or qualities, of an image; (2) *image analysis*—operations that produce numeric information based on an image; and (3) *image coding*—operations that code an image into a new form. By breaking down operations into these categories, the study of image processing becomes more structured in an applications sense. By exploring these three operational areas of image processing, we set forth the groundwork for studying the application and implementation of digital image processing.

IMAGE QUALITY ENHANCEMENT

Image quality enhancement operations serve to enhance or in some way alter the qualities of an image. The desired result is an image of improved quality. The improvement in the quality of an image is often subjective and is related to the application as well as the judgment of the viewer. For instance, one application may require the sharpening of an image that appears blurred. Another application, however, may defocus an image so that sharp details are eliminated, making other features of the image more detectable. The applications are different, making each viewer's operation appear contrary to the other's interest. In short, one viewer's enhancement is another's degradation.

The product of a quality enhancement operation is an output image yielding a changed version of the original. These enhancements may be applied to images that are in some way degraded from what would be considered a "good" image. Alternatively, "good" images may be enhanced to produce output images that show certain features enhanced for easier viewing. In either case, the qualities of the original image are altered in some way, affecting the image's appearance to the viewer.

Image quality enhancements may be either subjective or objective. Subjective enhancements are used to make an image more visually appealing and may be applied until an image achieves this goal. Objective enhancement, however,

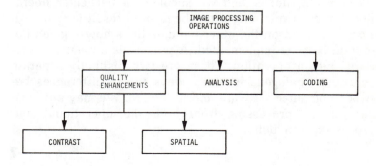

Figure 2-1 Operational breakdown of the image processing field.

corrects an image for known degradations and does not necessarily attempt to make the image more appealing. An example of objective quality enhancement is photometric correction, which will be discussed in Chapter 5. For the most part, we will discuss image quality enhancement in the subjective enhancement context.

Image quality enhancement operations may be conveniently broken into two subclasses, contrast and spatial enhancements. Contrast enhancements deal with the alteration of brightness within an image. Blacks, whites, and grays may be intensified or even suppressed, bringing out facets that were hard to see in the original. Spatial enhancements modify the content of detail within an image. Edges, for instance, may be accentuated, making viewing more appealing. A wide variety of contrast and spatial enhancements allow the viewer flexibility in the total modification or correction of an image.

The Human Visual System. When attempting the improvement of an image's quality, a knowledge of the characteristics of the human visual system is an important prerequisite. All images are ultimately processed by the visual system prior to the viewer's mental perception of them. An understanding of this fact not only helps us to define an image processing operation for maximum effectiveness, but also serves to indicate the limitations of the eye-brain system itself.

The eye is a complex unit that converts visual information into nerve impulses used by the brain to form a perceived image. The major functional components of the eye are illustrated in Figure 2-2. Light rays generated by a scene are collected by the *lens* and projected upon the surface of the *retina*. The *iris* serves to control the amount of light allowed to pass through the lens. The lens and iris are both physically protected by the *cornea*.

The retina is composed of light-sensitive elements known as *rods* and *cones*. On the order of 100 million of these *photoreceptors* serve to translate light intensity to nerve impulses. These impulses travel from the eye to the brain through nerve fibers within the *optic nerve*. The brain, in turn, deciphers the nerve impulse information to form what we perceive as an image.

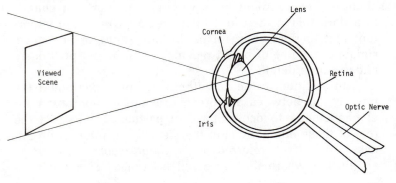

Figure 2-2 The human eye.

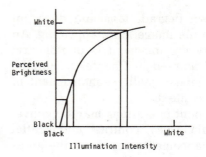

Figure 2-3 Typical logarithmic curve, similar to that of the eye's light intensity response.

Figure 2-4 Step gray scale with equal intensity steps.

Figure 2-5
Step gray scale with exponential intensity steps (equal perceived brightness steps).

What's interesting about the visual system is the way in which the photoreceptors respond to light intensity changes and interact with one another. With an understanding of these characteristics, we may better attack the problem of what constitutes image quality enhancement.

The impulses generated by the photoreceptors are then translated by the brain into perceived brightness. Research in this area of the visual system has shown that the relationship between impinging light upon a receptor and perceived brightness is not a linear function. This means that as the illumination intensity of a viewed object is changed, the viewer will not perceive an equal change in brightness. The actual response is logarithmic, appearing as a curve similar to that shown in Figure 2-3. In the dark regions, a slight illumination increase results in a large increase in perceived brightness. On the other hand, the same slight illumination increase in the bright regions yields a small increase in perceived brightness. The logarithmic response of the eye may be illustrated by Figures 2-4 and 2-5. In Figure 2-4, the brightness is incremented in equal illumination intensity steps from black to white. As we would expect from the graph in Figure 2-3, the dark regions are clustered at the left. The equal steps in the bright regions are virtually undetectable, making the entire right side appear white. Figure 2-5, however, illustrates intensities that are incremented in exponential steps, counteracting the eye's logarithmic response. The net result is a black-to-white transition that is perceived as happening in equal, or linear, steps.

The bottom line of the eye's logarithmic response is that sensitivity in the dark regions of a viewed scene is much greater than that of bright regions. This is because a change of equal intensity is perceived as a greater change in a dark region than in a bright region. This is an important fact to remember, for in the processing of an image, simple darkening of bright regions can bring out previously undetectable detail.

In addition to the logarithmic response characteristic, interactions between photoreceptors cause important visual phenomena to occur. Two, in particular, illustrate the role of these interactions in the visual perception of brightness. One effect, referred to as *simultaneous contrast*, is an illusion where the perceived brightness of a region is

10

dependent on the intensity of the surrounding area. This effect is shown in Figure 2-6. The two squares are of the same intensity, but the one on the left appears brighter, due to its darker background. (Conversely, the square on the right appears darker because of its lighter background.) The visual system apparently adjusts its brightness response based on the average intensity of the viewed scene. Since the left side has an overall darker average intensity than the right side, the perceived brightness is increased. (Likewise, the perceived brightness of the right side is decreased.) Hence, the difference in the apparent brightnesses of the two squares becomes apparent.

A second phenomenon, known as the *Mach band effect*, causes sharp intensity changes to be accentuated by the visual system. Figure 2-7 shows a sharp black-to-white transition along with the plots of actual brightness and perceived brightness change. The viewer sees a darker bar just to the left of the transition. Similarly, a lighter bar appears just to the right. These under- and overshoots are an artifact of the visual system. In fact, it turns out that without these additions, the transition does not appear nearly as sharp and crisp. The visual system actually adds these edge enhancements, sharpening everything we view. Figure

Figure 2-6 Simultaneous contrast —the two squares are the same intensity.

Figure 2-7
(a) Mach band effect —a dark band to the left and bright band to the right of the brightness transition may be seen.

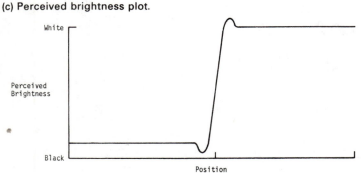

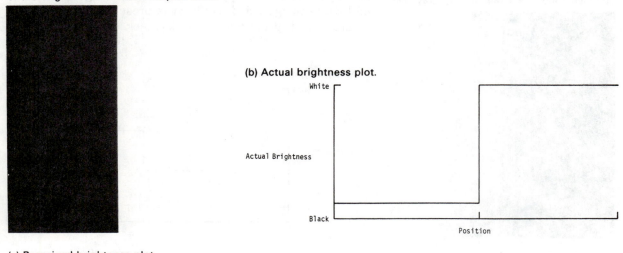

(b) Actual brightness plot.

(c) Perceived brightness plot.

2-8 illustrates this effect upon a stair-step intensity increase.

Intensity response characteristics may be combined with photoreceptor interaction properties. The visual system responds to transitions within a scene depending on the amount of light intensity change present. Slowly varying transitions are detectable even when composed of only small-intensity changes, whereas very minute transitions must contain large-intensity changes before they are seen. This means that highly detailed regions of an image composed of subtle intensity changes may be rendered undetected. Increasing the intensity change, or contrast, can make these details visible. The visual system is most responsive to scene details of high contrast.

These visual phenomena indicate complex processes occurring within the human visual system. By using knowledge of the system's response and interactive characteristics, we may better apply image processing operations, yielding more natural contrast and spatial enhancements.

Contrast Degradations/Enhancements. Contrast degradations in an image are problems associated with poor brightness characteristics. The term *contrast* deals with the distribution of brightness within an image. An image may be said to exhibit poor contrast if either low- or high-contrast attributes are apparent, neither of which are generally considered visually appealing. When dealing with black-and-white images, high contrast is present when an image is composed primarily of dark black and bright white

Figure 2-8
(a) Mach band effect seen in step gray scale.

(b) Actual brightness plot.

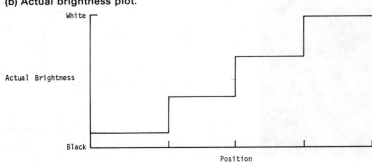

(c) Perceived brightness plot.

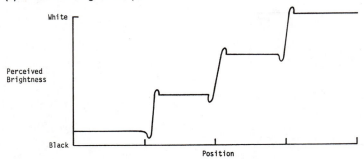

tones. Scene details are made up of harsh black-to-white transitions rather than the more natural, smooth gray tones. The appearance of a high-contrast image is that of intense boldness. Low-contrast images, on the other hand, are characterized by a washed-out look. Only middle gray tones exist, with dark black and bright white tones virtually nonexistent. Scene details appear subdued, making the viewing of such images difficult.

A well-balanced image of "good" contrast is composed of gray tones stretching from the dark blacks, through the grays, to the bright whites. Operations to correct an image of either low or high contrast are relatively simple. The results of these operations are corrected images where the overall gray tone balance is restored to a more natural distribution.

In contrast enhancement, simply achieving "good" image contrast is not always the ultimate goal. These techniques may further be used to make visible some aspect of the image that was previously hidden. In this type of enhancement, a resulting image of very high contrast, or other characteristic, may be desired. The results of these operations do not always yield aesthetically pleasing images but rather amplify some feature of interest.

Contrast enhancements are common image processing operations used to alter the overall brightness qualities of an image. They may be used to correct contrast deficiencies or to extract feature information not evident in the original.

Spatial Degradations/Enhancements. Spatial degradations in an image are problems associated with the presentation of image scene details. The term *spatial* deals with the two-dimensional nature of an image scene. An image may be said to exhibit poor spatial qualities if detailed areas are blurred or not well defined. Often edge details, such as black-to-white transitions, may be blurred, not exhibiting the sharp qualities generally associated with them. These types of spatial problems may be corrected or at least improved upon by relatively straightforward operations. The results are images in which spatial detail is restored to more accurately represent the detail of the original scene.

Additional spatial degradations include image noise, such as "snow" in a television image. Image scene geometric distortions also fall in this category.

As in contrast enhancement, correcting an image to a visually pleasing form is not always the pursued objective. Sometimes it is desired to enhance spatial details to an extreme, making object structure features more visible. Edge enhancement, where only object edge details are highlighted, is a common enhancement processing task.

Spatial enhancements are used to alter the spatial detail qualities of an image. They are often employed not only for image degradation correction but also in the extraction of object features not visible in the original.

IMAGE ANALYSIS

Image analysis operations produce nonpictorial results. Instead, the output is numeric or graphic information based on characteristics of the original image, with the objective of describing some aspect of the image and presenting the results to the viewer. Image analysis operations serve to describe image qualities, assisting in enhancement operations. Furthermore, descriptions of image scene features, automatic scene object measurements, and pattern recognition are all common analysis operations.

The most common analysis operation encountered in general image processing is that of the image histogram. The histogram relates, in bar graph form, the brightness distribution present in an image. Contrast information may be readily obtained from this graph, allowing the appropriate enhancement operation to be chosen. The brightness and contrast measurement given by the histogram is invaluable when attempting to correct an image for these degradations.

Aside from image quality measurements, analysis operations are most prevalent in automatic control applications. Such uses include the automatic dimensional measurement and classification of parts fabricated on an assembly line, automated security systems where certain known violations are watched for within a live video image, and remote sensing where aerial Earth images may be broken into various geological categories and tabulated for resource studies.

IMAGE CODING

The final class of image processing operations is that of image coding. These operations serve to reduce the amount of information necessary to describe an image. Two types of coding exist. The first codes an image in such a way that no information is lost. The reconstruction of the original image may be obtained uniquely from the coded version. The second codes an image into an abridged form. An example of abridged image coding would be to break the image into primitive subparts, or structures, coding only the location and orientation of each piece. While the second approach yields a considerably larger data reduction factor, the reconstructed image will often be far from an exact representation of the original. The choice of the coding scheme to be used is determined, as usual, by the application.

Reasons for using image coding lie particularly in the applications of image transmission and storage. Both make use of a limited medium and are therefore made more efficient through coding techniques. For instance, coding images into reduced forms allows either more image data to be transmitted in a given period of time or more to be stored in a given segment of a storage device. Image cod-

14

ing relates directly to conservation of equipment resources, particularly in bulk applications.

Processing Classification

The act of carrying out a computational operation is called a *process*. More specifically, the term *frame process* refers to an operation applied to an image frame, where *image frame* is simply a term used to denote an image in its entirety. All image processing operations may be said to be implemented through the use of a frame process. In the most general case, a frame process would be written in software and executed by a computer having access to the image data.

Previously, we broke the general field of image processing into three operational categories. The categories— quality enhancement, analysis, and coding—served to isolate these primary endeavors of research and application in such a way that each could be handled as a separate area of study. Although each plays a major role, we are primarily interested in quality enhancement. This is because most all images processed undergo some sort of quality enhancement either prior to or following other applied processes.

Because image quality enhancement operations are so popular, the most attention has been given to them. Image processing systems tend to support the enhancement operations to a higher level than the others. Also, since a fixed set of enhancements are often carried out on large sequences of related images, the speed with which the operation is carried out becomes of interest. For this reason, image processing systems often incorporate special-purpose hardware that allow the fast execution of certain families of enhancement operations.

In digital image processing, two processes are broken out of the general class of frame processing to be handled by high-speed hardware. These subsets are known as *point and group processes*. They serve to implement contrast and spatial enhancements, respectively. Furthermore, point processes are comprised of two parts—single image and dual image. The single image process allows standard contrast enhancements, while the dual image process adds the capability of combining multiple images. This overall process breakdown is illustrated in Figure 2-9.

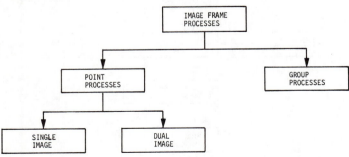

Figure 2-9 Process breakdown of image processing operations.

Implementation of point and group processes in special-purpose hardware allows the image quality enhancements to be handled expediently. Because of the predominant use of these operations, the overall image processing system throughout is increased as a result.

Generally, when speaking of a frame process, we are referring to a process other than the defined point or group process subsets. Using this premise, all image processing operations may be implemented through the use of one of four processes. The two point processes along with the group process provide for the bulk of image quality enhancements and are handled by high-speed hardware processors. The remaining operations involving other quality enhancements along with image analysis and coding are handled through the use of frame processes. Frame processes are generally executed through software programs by a host computer.

Part II of this book develops the above processing concepts. The reader will ultimately be armed with the knowledge to configure and execute image operations based on the requirements of a particular application.

The Processing System

A digital image processing system is a collection of hardware devices providing the digitization, storage, display, and processing of digital images. It is this system that yields the means of implementing a process upon a stored image. Figure 2-10 illustrates the common structure of a general purpose system.

The first order of business in any image processing system is to digitize an image. Most general-purpose systems will accept standard television video signals as inputs. The input device is normally a video camera imaging the scene of interest, whether live or a photographic print. The act of digitizing converts the analog electrical form of the video image into a digital form that may be stored in a digital memory device. Once the image exists in digital

Figure 2-10 Basic image processing system.

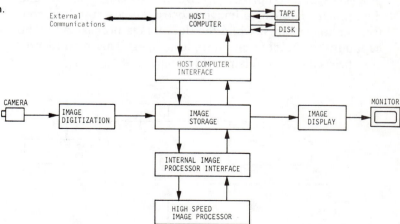

memory, we are able to freeze it for subsequent display and processing.

The display of an image residing in memory is accomplished by repetitively reading the digital image data out to a display subsystem. Here, image data are reconverted to the standard television format and displayed on a television monitor. Once an image is brought into the image memory it is continuously displayed on the monitor.

The overseer of the image processing system is the host computer system. The host controls the system, deciding when to digitize, display, and process an image. The host also serves as the user's interface to the system. The host system, through the host computer interface, has direct access to the image memory such that it may carry out image processing tasks. Additionally, the host may transfer image data to and from long-term storage devices such as magnetic disk or tape. For small image processing systems, the host is often a microcomputer.

The final element of the digital image processing system is that of a high-speed image processor. Although the host computer has the ability to carry out any definable process upon a stored image, its speed of execution can be relatively slow. It becomes desirable to implement common image processes in hardware so that their execution time is reduced to a minimum. As mentioned earlier, the point and group processes are frequently handled in hardware. These processes allow the user the ability to modify image contrast and spatial attributes, as well as combine multiple images in an expedient manner. Since quality enhancement operations are most commonly used, added hardware can greatly augment the performance of the image processing system.

Part III of this book explores the basic configuration and design of the components of a general image processing system. Assuming reasonable skills in digital circuit design, the reader will gain the knowledge to configure and design a basic system.

PROCESSING CONCEPTS ||||

The Digital Image

Digital image processing, by definition, operates upon pictorial information of a digital form. The conversion of every day images into this form is the most preliminary operation to occur prior to digital processing. Images of interest may be derived from a variety of sources: photographs, television, radar, scanning infrared detectors, acoustics, or X-rays—the list is virtually endless. No matter what the origin, however, the image must ultimately be placed into a format that the digital processor understands.

In general, digital image processing is carried out on standard television format images, because of the widespread standardization and acceptance throughout several related industries. In addition, almost any image may easily be converted to this format. From this point on we will assume all our processing to be carried out on standard black-and-white television images, with only brief departures to consider the differences in processing color images.

Let us now explore the terms, conventions, and format of the digital image.

Forming a Digital Image

A typical black-and-white photograph is composed of shades of gray spanning from black to white, and is known as a *continuous tone* image. This means that the various

21

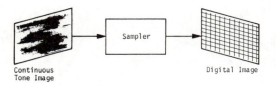

Continuous
Tone Image

Sampler

Digital Image

Figure 3-1 Conversion from continuous tone to digital image.

shades of gray blend together with no disruption to faithfully reproduce the elements of the original scene. The digital image processor, on the other hand, must work with discrete pieces of data on a one-by-one basis. To convert our continuous tone image to a digital image we must chop it into individual points of information. This "chopping" is referred to as *digitizing* or, more properly, *sampling*, because we are taking samples of the brightness of the photograph at specific locations within it. Each sample is given a numeric value based on its brightness, ranging from black through the grays to white. Additionally, each sample is assigned coordinates describing its location within the image. A sample is often referred to as a picture element, or *pixel*, because of its representation of a discrete element of the digital image.

An image is digitized into a square grid of pixels, each of which is labeled with a pair of coordinates—one defining the column that it is in and one the row. Column numbers range from 0, at the left-most side, to *n*, where *n* is the number of columns in the image. Likewise, rows are assigned numbers from 0, at the top-most side, to *m* where *m* is the number of rows in the image. As an example, the pixel with coordinates (200, 150) resides at the crossing point of column 200, row 150. To make better sense and (as we will see later) to conform more with television standards, the row coordinate is referred to as the *line* number and the column the *pixel* number in that line. This sampled image numbering convention is illustrated in Figure 3-2.

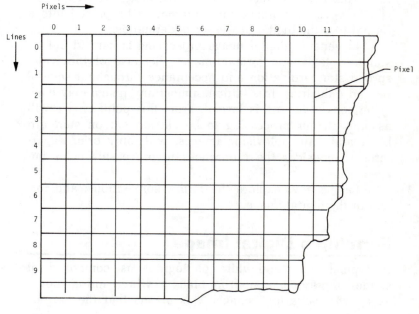

Figure 3-2 The discrete pixel numbering convention.

Our image has now been divided into individual, discrete points of information. Furthermore, each point has a defined location within the image, its coordinates, and a brightness value associated with it.

When dealing with the digitization of an image, there is always the question of how good the representation is when compared with the original. We define the limitations of the digitization process with the term *resolution.* Resolution is the separation of something into its basic subparts. In image processing, resolution may be broken into two definite types, *spatial* and *brightness,* with a third type, *frame rate,* playing a role not directly related to the visual appearance of an image.

Spatial Resolution

The term *spatial* refers to the concept of space, in our case a two-dimensional space. Our two-dimensional object is an image with a fixed height and width. When we speak of *spatial resolution,* we are describing how many pixels our digital image is divided into. Simply put, the finer this resolution is, the closer we approach the spatial appearance of the original image.

Optimally, we wish to digitize an image such that no information is lost in the translation from the original image to the digital image. This means that a properly displayed digital image will be identical to the original to an observer. In order to better understand the criteria for establishing the necessary number of samples required in a digital image, we must introduce the concept of *spatial frequency.* Any image contains scene detail in varying degrees. For example, details may range from the minutely detailed hairs on a person's head to the smoothly varying shades in the contours of the face. In quantifying this visual detail, we speak of spatial frequency or the rate at which brightness of an image changes from dark to light.

As an example of spatial frequency content in an image, let us examine the details present in Figure 3-3. If we look at a single line of the image as it crosses through varying details of the scene, the brightness of the scene encountered on the left half of the highlighted line is found to be erratic. These rapid changes in brightness are said to contain high spatial frequency. On the right side of the line, however, slowly varying shades of gray are observed. This portion is said to contain low spatial frequency. We must remember that when looking at a line of image we are actually only considering one-dimensional spatial frequency components. Spatial resolution takes into account the rate of change of brightness in an image going from left to right as well as top to bottom.

To make a decision about the necessary sampling rate needed to properly resolve an image, we use the classical *Nyquist Criterion,* also known as the Sampling Theo-

Figure 3-3
(a) A scene of varying spatial frequency detail.

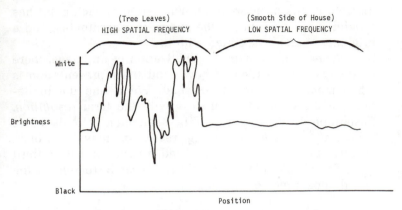

(b) Brightness plot along highlighted line.

rem. This theory tells us in mathematical terms that to fully represent the rate of brightness change, or detail, in an original image we must sample it at a rate at least twice as high as the highest spatial frequency of the detail. In other words, if a particular detail in an original image varies from dark to light within a certain distance, our samples, or pixels, must be fine enough so that two of them fall upon the detail itself. It is also true that it becomes useless and wasteful to sample an image at a rate any faster than twice its maximum spatial frequency content. This may be further refined to say it is wasteful to sample at a rate faster than twice that of the finest detail *wished to be resolved in the digital image.* Some applications do not require that all details be present in the digitized image. Keep in mind, though, that once an image is digitized with a limit on the sampling frequency, the lost detail is gone forever.

At this point, we are ready to discuss spatial resolution of a digital image. The name of the game here is to take an image from a source, such as a photograph, and break it into enough discrete pixels so that the eye can detect no difference between the digitized image and the original. Figure 3-4 shows an image digitized to various spatial resolutions. The 32 line × 32 pixel image shows obvious coarseness where detail has been lost by the pixel "blocking" effect. As spatial resolution increases, the image looks more and more natural. A television, in fact, has 485 visible lines per image and the equivalent of roughly 380 pixels per line. Viewing the picture from a reasonable distance makes it difficult for the viewer to see any lines at all. However, up close, the lines are clearly visible. The chosen spatial resolution of a digital image must take into account three factors—the detail in the original to be seen in the digital image, the displayed size of the digital image, and the viewer's distance from it. As a rather gross exam-

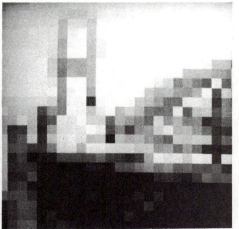

Figure 3-4
(a) Image of 256 × 256 spatial resolution. (b) 128 × 128.

(c) 64 × 64. (d) 32 × 32.

ple, digitization of an image for use in a movie requires on the order of a 4,000 line × 7,500 pixel image so that when displayed on a standard movie screen, considerably enlarged from the original, the viewer does not see the individual pixel composition.

The distance that an image appears from its observer directly determines how much scene detail will be visible. For instance, a photograph held twelve inches from an observer will show considerably more detail than when held five feet away. Therefore, as the display-observer distance is increased, spatial resolution in the image may be decreased. Looking at the images in Figure 3-4, we see that the visible pixel "blocking" effect diminishes as the images are pulled farther and farther away from the eye. The display-observer viewing geometry is depicted in Figure 3-5. As the distance is doubled, so may the size of the observed display increase without any detectable spatial detail loss to the observer.

In practice, it is sometimes prohibitive to actually implement the spatial resolution required by the above con-

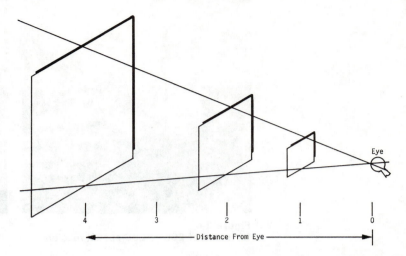

Eye

4   3   2   1   0

◄——————— Distance From Eye ———————►

Figure 3-5 The display-observer viewing geometry.

siderations. This is because storage of the image in computer memory becomes unmanageable, while increased computational time required to process the image becomes undesirable. So, as in most endeavors, we are faced with a tradeoff, image resolution presented to the observer versus computer memory storage space and processing time.

It has become somewhat of a standard among image processor equipment manufacturers to chose a spatial resolution of 512 $\times$ 512 to be compatible with television formats. You will note that a resolution of 512 $\times$ 512 and not 485 $\times$ 380 is selected. This is because 512 is an even power of 2, a number convenient to the computer and digital processing hardware world. It should be noted that other resolutions are also common. 1024 $\times$ 1024 is often found in high-resolution applications where high detail must be resolved accurately within an image. On the other hand, 256 $\times$ 256 is quite acceptable for general use in education, machine process control, hobby, and many other applications. Once again, an image of any of these spatial resolutions is acceptable to the viewer when observed from an appropriate distance. All images appearing in this book are 256 $\times$ 256.

There is one other topic worth mentioning with regard to spatial resolution, the concept of *aliasing*. The phenomenon of aliasing has to do with the erroneous representation of original-image, high-frequency detail within the digitized image. Aliasing appears when the Nyquist Criterion is violated for a given spatial frequency present in the original image. This occurs when a detail within a scene has a spatial frequency greater than half the sampling frequency. In this case, the detail is said to be *undersampled*. The high-frequency detail ends up being translated to a lower frequency because some of the brightness transitions are missed in the sampling process. This is illustrated in Figure 3-6. When aliasing occurs, moiré patterns may appear in the digitized image. Unless an image of very repetitive high-frequency detail is undersampled, though, the effect of aliasing may generally be disregarded.

26

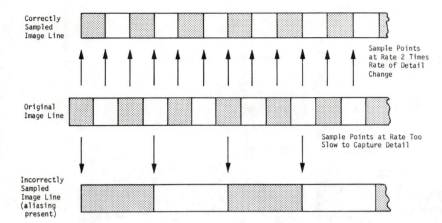

Figure 3-6 The aliasing effect when undersampling is present.

Brightness Resolution

The second resolution concerning digital images is that of *brightness*. As covered in the previous section, every pixel represents the brightness of the original image at the point of its sampling. The concept of *brightness resolution* is concerned with how accurately the digital pixel brightness compares to the original brightness at the same location in the image.

The digitizing process samples the original image at predetermined grid locations. Each sample brightness is then converted to an integer numeric value; this is known as *quantization*. The quantization operation converts an analog brightness level at a sample point to a numeric value within a certain accuracy tolerance, or brightness resolution. This process is carried out by an Analog-to-Digital, or A/D, converter and will be discussed in Chapter 6.

In quantizing the brightness of a pixel, we must first define to what accuracy the conversion will be made. For instance, conversion to a three-bit binary number allows each pixel to be represented by one of eight brightness levels. These levels are represented digitally by the binary numbers 000, 001, 010, 011, 100, 101, 110, and 111, spanning in brightness from black to white. The eight levels of brightness comprise what is called a *gray scale*, or in this case, the three-bit gray scale. Clearly evident in the three-bit gray scale, shown in Figure 3-7, are the eight distinct levels of brightness. Each brightness is easily discernable by the eye. Figure 3-8 shows an image quantized to brightness resolutions from one to six bits. Figure 3-9 breaks an image of six-bit brightness resolution into separate "bit-plane" images, illustrating the impact of each bit on the overall image.

We must pay attention to the number of levels of gray available to the brightness quantizer. As seen, the lower brightness resolution images allow the quantization to be visible to the eye. Increasing the number of bits representing brightness expands the gray scale so that it blends together more undetectably. For each added bit in

Figure 3-7 The 3-bit gray scale.

Figure 3-8
(a) Image of 6 bit = 64 gray levels res

(b) 5 bit = 32 gray levels.

(c) 4 bit = 16 gray levels.

(d) 3 bit = 8 gray levels.

(e) 2 bit = 4 gray levels.

(f) 1 bit = 2 gray levels.

Figure 3-9
(a) Image bit planes, bit 6 (most significant bit).

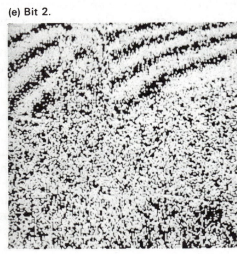

(b) Bit 5.

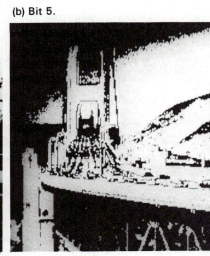

(c) Bit 4.

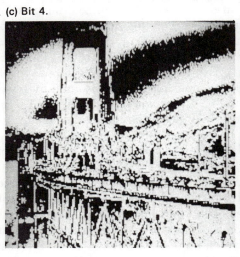

(d) Bit 3.

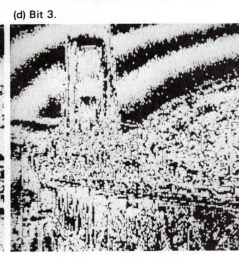

(e) Bit 2.

(f) Bit 1 (least significant bit).

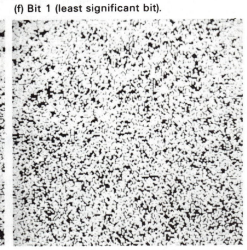

the conversion, the brightness resolution of the gray scale is doubled.

Referring back to the two-bit image in Figure 3-8, we see the effect of the phenomenon known as *contouring*. Contouring occurs because of limited quantization—all pixels are allowed to fall within one of only four brightnesses. The continuous tone quality of the original is limited, making areas of the digital image abruptly change from one gray level to another, where the change was gradual in the original. Where resolution entered into detail representation in the spatial domain, it is contouring effects that are to be minimized by appropriate resolution in the brightness domain.

Before making the final decision of how many bits to assign to the gray scale, we must touch on the response characteristics of the eye. As we saw in Chapter 2, the eye is much more sensitive to intensity changes in dark regions of an image than in bright regions. The eye responds logarithmically to intensity change. This means that contouring may be visible in dark areas of a digitized image when not evident in lighter areas. For this reason, it is often beneficial to quantize brightness on a logarithmic scale rather than a linear scale. This means that the dark, or low-brightness areas, will be represented by more gray levels, leaving the high-brightness areas represented by fewer.

The logarithmic gray scale buys us the ability to place finer brightness resolution in the low end of the gray scale, where the eye is most sensitive to intensity change. In effect, we have linearized the response of the eye by making the gray scale logarithmic.

Image processor equipment manufacturers have generally adopted 8-bit logarithmic gray scales to represent digitized images. The 8-bit quantization assures no detectable change from one gray level to an adjacent one, where logarithmic quantization takes advantage of the response characteristics of the eye. For low-end user applications such as amateur radio, computer hobbyism, and some machine process control, 6-bit, 4-bit, and even lower gray scales are often acceptable. Additionally, linear quantization is often not a drawback for these uses. Because of the difficult hardware implications, we will limit our discussions in this book to an 8-bit linear gray scale.

Frame Rate

A more subtle form of resolution manifests itself in the image processor hardware display of digital images. With the normal display mode being that of a television-type device, we are interested in the rate at which the image is updated, known as *frame rate*. Commercial television updates its image entirely, using a technique called interlacing, every 1/30 of a second with little flicker observable to the viewer. Reducing flickering in a displayed image is important when viewer fatigue is of concern.

The use of standard television monitors is common in image processing, where the frame update rate of 30 times per second produces little distraction to the viewer. Because of this, most image processing equipment is designed around the commercial television standard. The standard calls for refreshing the displayed image in an *interlaced* format every 1/30 of a second. Interlacing gives the impression to the observer that a new frame is present every 1/60 of a second.

High-end image processors will often raise the frame rate to 1/100 of a second. The result is a rock-steady image display. This requires the use of higher-speed image memory and special-purpose display monitors. We will dwell on the standard 1/30 of a second interlace scheme. This approach is more conventional, especially when dealing with a standard television camera input, as we will.

Interlacing, frame rate, and spatial and brightness resolutions are discussed in Chapter 6, where the standard television video format is overviewed.

The Histogram

Image analysis operations deal with the generation of numerical descriptions of various image characteristics. An important class of these operations is used in the analysis of image degradations prior to enhancement. In particular, contrast attributes of an image are of major interest, giving a good overall quality assessment. A tool, known as the *image histogram,* gives us a concise, easy-to-read measure of this important parameter. In general terms, a histogram is defined as a frequency distribution graph of a set of numbers. Our special version is the gray level histogram, giving us a graphical representation of how many pixels within an image fall into the various gray level boundaries.

A histogram appears as a graph with "brightness" on the horizontal axis from 0 to 255 (for an 8-bit gray scale), and "number of pixels" on the vertical axis. To find the number of pixels having a particular brightness within an image, we simply look up the brightness on the horizontal axis, follow up the graph bar and read off the number of pixels on the vertical axis. Since all pixels must have some brightness defining them, adding the number of pixels in each brightness column will sum to the total number of pixels in the image.

The histogram gives us a convenient, easy-to-read representation of the concentration of pixels versus brightness in an image. Using this graph we are able to see immediately whether the image is basically dark or light and high or low contrast. Furthermore, it gives us our first clues as to what contrast enhancements would be appropriately applied to make the image more subjectively pleasing to an observer.

Contrast/Dynamic Range Indication

A term often used in describing an image of any sort is *contrast*. We intuitively understand contrast to mean how dull or sharp an image appears with respect to gray tones. Contrast in an image is clearly illustrated in the histogram. Low contrast appears as a mound of pixel brightnesses in the gray scale leaving other gray regions completely unoccupied. High contrast shows up as a bimodal histogram where two peaks exist at the outer brightness regions. We see that by "reading" the histogram, contrast parameters become evident, allowing us to further pursue the correct contrast enhancement approach. A well-balanced image is generally characterized by medium, or "good" contrast.

Dynamic range is a measure of how wide the occupied portion of the gray scale is. For instance, a mound of pixels falling between gray values 50 and 100 (within a range of 0 to 255), with none in the other regions, indicates a small dynamic range of brightness, whereas a wide gray scale distribution shows large dynamic range. An image with small dynamic range does not occupy all the available spread of gray values; the image has really only been quantized to a gray scale comprised of the occupied range. This indicates low brightness resolution along with low contrast. Large dynamic range generally implies a well-balanced image except if it is a bimodal distribution, in which case the image is high contrast. Three common histograms, along with their original images, are illustrated in Figures 4-1 through 4-3.

Figure 4-1

(a) Low contrast/low dynamic range image.

(b) The histogram.

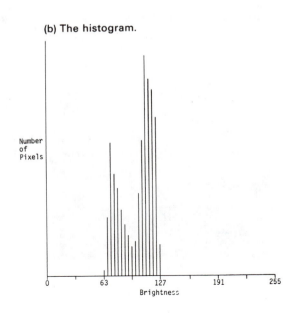

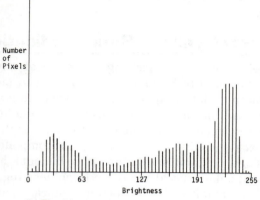

Figure 4-2
(a) High contrast/high dynamic range image.

(b) The histogram.

It should be noted that natural images generally are characterized by wide dynamic range and medium contrast. However, this is not always the case. It just may be the attributes of the original scene that dictate departures from a well-balanced image. Often, though, even if the original had low contrast or low dynamic range, a corrected version will be more appealing to the viewer.

Manipulation Effects

In dealing with the image degradations evidenced by the histogram, we will now touch on basic histogram manipulation, which will be discussed in more detail in Chapter 5. Two modifications are commonly implemented: *histogram sliding* and *histogram stretching*. These operations are meant to redistribute the histogram so that contrast and

Figure 4-3
(a) Good contrast/high dynamic range image.

(b) The histogram.

34

dynamic range may be enhanced. Given the low contrast image and histogram of Figure 4-1 we see that the pixel gray scale distribution is clumped in one area of the graph. Not only is low contrast indicated here, but also low dynamic range. By sliding the "clump" to the left and then stretching it out to the right we effect a higher contrast and wider dynamic range. This makes the image better balanced and more natural as a result.

The sliding operation is simply the addition or subtraction of a constant brightness to all pixels in the image. A pixel of brightness 20 attains a brightness of 30 when 10 is added. Doing this to every pixel effectively slides the entire graph to the right by 10 gray levels. The basic effect of sliding is a lightening or darkening of the image.

Histogram stretching is the multiplication of all pixels in the image by a constant value. A histogram, with all pixels residing in the left half, will be spread out to occupy the entire gray scale range when multiplied by a constant of 2. This operation stretches the contrast and dynamic range of an image.

There exists an interesting point concerning the stretching of a low dynamic range image. In an image in which the histogram shows all pixels falling in the left half, only half of the gray levels are actually used. Although the image appears dark, we may stretch the histogram to make the distribution span the entire range. Dynamic range is increased—which is desired—but there are still only half the number of allowable gray levels occupied. (Remember, there were only half to begin with.) Where the original pixels fell, the original brightness resolution was maintained, but the image appeared dark. Now the stretching operation has stretched the original gray values to twice the range by skipping every other gray value in the case of multiplying by two. We have not lost brightness resolution, merely redistributed the original information.

Object Classification

Elementary classification of objects within an image scene is sometimes feasible through histogram analysis. The beach scene, illustrated in Figure 4-4, is primarily composed of four basic elements—white water, sky, calm water, and rocks. Each of the elements tend to be comprised of gray levels different from one another. What we are able to do is carry out a classification of scene objects based on their gray level compositions. Looking at the image histogram, the four regions of gray level concentration are seen as distinct peaks separated by valleys. For classification, the histogram may be broken into the four gray level regions, each labeled for the objects represented. Using a simple pixel point process (to be covered in Chapter 5), we may generate an image where only four gray levels appear, each representing one of the four classified ob-

Figure 4-4
(a) Original beach scene.

(b) The histogram broken into four brightness classes.

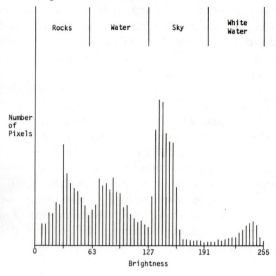

(c) The original scene classified by use of four gray levels.

(d) Class 1—white water.

(e) Class 2—sky.

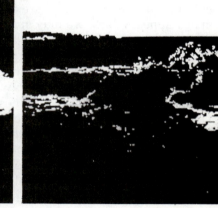

(f) Class 3—calm water.

(g) Class 4—rocks.

jects. Furthermore, four independent images may be generated, each highlighting the objects of one classification category.

Like all processing of data, there is a drawback, or undesirable artifact, to this technique. Objects in a scene may be composed of gray level regions that overlap, objects will then have portions that fall in another's classification. Additionally, unclassified areas may have pixels spanning the gray scale. Those pixels are then improperly classified as belonging to certain object groups.

The histogram object classification operation is basic. It works best on simple scenes with objects that have distinctly different gray scale occupancies. However, in certain applications, the simplicity of this technique may be exactly what is called for.

Picture Operations

We touched on various processing fundamentals in Chapter 2. Remember that all operations of interest to us fell within four process categories: point processing with one image, point processing with two images, group processing, and frame processing. These categories—though broad in an applications sense—each relate to a fundamental operation, with the exception of frame processing, which is meant to classify various functions not included in point or group processing.

Throughout this chapter, reference to Image Operation Studies will be made when appropriate. These studies are compiled in Part IV, "Processing in Action," and are provided to consolidate the image operations introduced in this chapter. It should be noted that the processing techniques presented here are not meant to represent an exhaustive study of image processing capabilities. Rather, they represent an overview of the most commonly used processes. The hope is that the reader will become sufficiently stimulated to gain any required depth in the field through additional studies. Good references to these topics include Further Reading/References I-1 through I-8.

In Chapter 3, a pixel within an image was spatially located by its line and pixel coordinates. Using the Cartesian coordinate system, the pixel coordinate is represented by x and the line coordinate by y. For instance, the pixel located at the crossing point of line number 25 and pixel number 125 is denoted by the coordinates (125, 25). We take this convention a bit farther in this chapter, for we must now discriminate between input and output images.

An *input image* is defined as an image that is used as data to be processed. Any resulting image is referred to as an *output image*. So in calling out the coordinates of an image pixel, a prefix of either *I* or *O* is used to denote input or output image. Where multiple input images are used in an operation, a subscript may be appended to the *I* prefix.

The general case flow diagram of an image processing operation is depicted in Figure 5-1. Input images are denoted by $I_1(x,y)$ and $I_2(x,y)$. In an operation requiring a single input image, no subscript need be used. The output image, if present, is denoted by $O(x,y)$. This basic diagram provides the fundamental representation of all image processing operations.

A typical image processing system possessing reasonable image quality representation may be based on an image resolution of 256 × 256, quantized to 8 bits. We will dwell on these resolution parameters throughout the proceeding development of topics.

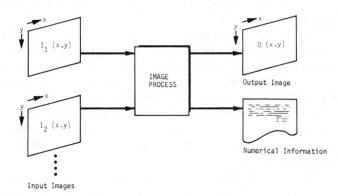

Input Images

Figure 5-1 The image operation flow diagram.

Pixel Point Processing/Single Image

Pixel point processing is the most fundamental class of image processing operations. Used primarily in contrast enhancement operations, the pixel point process is a simple yet invaluable tool. Point processes allow the alteration of pixel gray scale occupancy. On a one-by-one basis, the gray level of each pixel in the input image is modified, often by a mathematical or logical relationship, to a new value and placed in the output image at the same spatial location. All pixels are handled individually. For instance, the pixel at coordinates I(x,y) in the input image is modified and returned to the output image at coordinate $O(x,y)$. With this in mind, we note that point operations process pixel brightness attributes with no action on spatial attributes. Spatial processing, as we will see later, is handled by pixel group and frame processing.

The general equation for a point process is given by the equation

$$O(x,y) = M[I(x,y)]$$

where *M* is the *mapping function.* It is implied that all pixels in the input image are operated upon. This means that the brightness of an output pixel residing at coordinates (x,y) is equal to the brightness of the input pixel at coordinates (x,y) after being modified by the function M. We refer to the function *M* as the mapping function because it maps input brightnesses to output brightnesses.

As an example, suppose that we wish to make a negative image from a positive one. Here, just like a photographic negative, the blacks in the input image will become white, the whites black, and the grays in between take on their respective negative qualities. This operation, often referred to as the *complement image operation,* does prove useful. As we learned, the eye responds better to slight changes in contrast in dark regions of an image than in light regions. With this process, slight contrast changes in the bright areas in the input image, normally undetectable, are transformed into the dark regions in the output image where they now become visible.

Figure 5-2 illustrates this operation along with the mapping function. By locating the input pixel gray level on the map's horizontal axis, moving up to the map point and across to the vertical axis, we acquire the respective output gray level. As expected, black (0) maps to white (255) and vice versa. All of the intermediate gray levels are correspondingly mapped, yielding the final complemented image. Image Operation Study #5 provides additional insight into this operation.

The uses for point processing are vast. As mentioned in the previous chapter, histogram manipulation is carried out by a point process. This class of point processes is re-

Figure 5-2
(a) Original image.

(b) Complemented image.

(c) The complement operation mapping function.

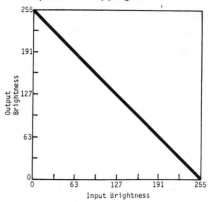

ferred to as *contrast enhancement.* Another operation
known as *photometric correction,* deals with the correction
of problems caused by photosensor incongruencies. One
such use corrects spacecraft image sensor nonlinearities
caused by size and weight constraints. The artist may
make use of point processing when developing silkscreen
overlays, graphics, and glass etching masks.

Point processing is a simple but truly fundamental element of digital image processing. No matter what type of
operation is employed upon an image, some form of point
processing is probably involved, even if it is used to simply
clean up undesired artifacts left behind by another process.

CONTRAST ENHANCEMENT

We discussed histogram sliding and stretching in Chapter
2; now we will fully describe the uses and effects of these
operations.

The first thing we do is generate a histogram of the
image to be processed. This charted pixel gray level distribution of an image will often tell us immediately where the
"sore" spots are. These troubled areas are expressed in
terms of contrast and dynamic range of the distribution.
Referring back to Figures 4-1 though 4-3, we see histograms
of images with varying qualities—low contrast/low dynamic range, high contrast/high dynamic range, and good
contrast/high dynamic range. These are the types of histograms most frequently encountered. By sliding and stretching the histograms, we may make an image of poor
contrast quality quite respectable.

Contrast enhancement is a point process involving
the addition, subtraction, multiplication, or division of a
constant value to every pixel within the image. The histogram is useful in determining the operations to be
employed and in measuring the accomplishments after-
ward.

Figure 5-3 illustrates an image progressing through the
contrast enhancement process. We see the original image
histogram displaying a mound of gray levels occupied in
the center. The image appears low in contrast. The enhancement of increased contrast may be accomplished by
first sliding the mound of gray levels down to the dark
area of the histogram. We do this by subtracting 60 from
each pixel's brightness, using a point process with the appropriate map. The resulting image yields no more contrast; we have simply relocated the pixel brightness range
so that the darkest pixels of the original are now actually
full black. Now comes the stretching. To make the mound
stretch the full range of grays we must multiply every
brightness by 2. Black (0) remains 0, because $0 \times 2 = 0$. A
pixel of brightness 10 becomes 20, and so forth, to the
maximum-valued pixel in the input image of 120 increasing

Figure 5-3
(a) Original low-contrast image.

(b) The histogram.

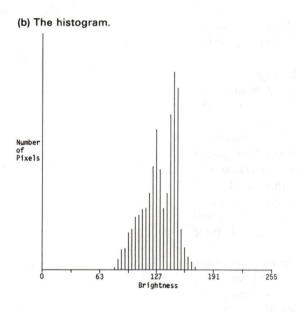

(c) Histogram slide map.

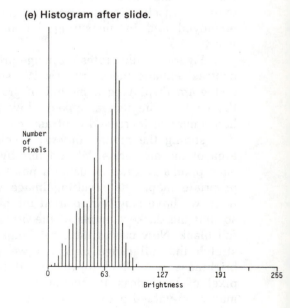

(d) Image after histogram slide.

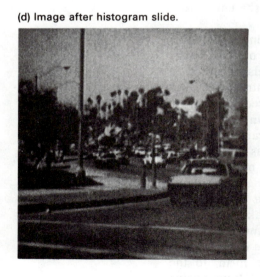

(e) Histogram after slide.

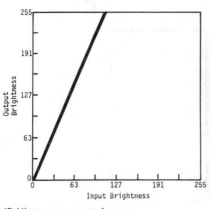

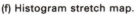

(f) Histogram stretch map.

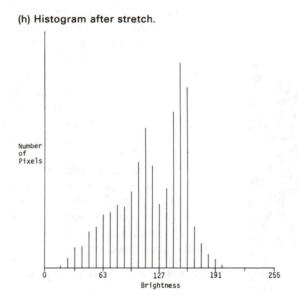

(g) Image after histogram stretch.

(h) Histogram after stretch.

to 240. 240 is virtually the limit of the 256-level gray scale. Again, a pixel process is used to effect the stretch. Our image now appears well balanced with good contrast characteristics. The final histogram shows the same. These contrast enhancement operations are further discussed in Image Operation Studies #2, #3 and #4.

All images may be operated on in the above manner to acquire histograms that appear well balanced. But what if the desired result is that of high contrast? Many times production of an image of obtuse appearance is desired in order to make some attribute clearer. In short, the subjective criteria on which an image is judged good or bad are based on its intended application.

Some images are very low in contrast as a function of their origin, such as a scene with poor lighting. An example of this is a low-light-level original in which only a few gray values separate background from object. Figure 5-4 shows an image of a road sign taken under these undesirable lighting conditions. In order to read the lettering clear-

43

Figure 5-4
(a) Original low-contrast, dark image.

(c) Output image with sign lettering highlighted.

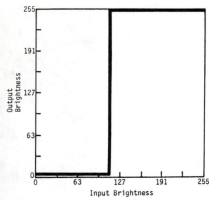

(b) Binary Contrast Enhancement map.

ly, we may implement what is known as a *binary contrast enhancement operation.* The mapping function illustrates that all pixels of brightness less than that of the chosen threshold brightness will be set to black (0), and those above will be set to white (255). By choosing the correct threshold value, we may force the lettering to go to white and the background to black. This is possible because in the original, the letters appear slightly brighter than the background. The processed image is characterized by sharply highlighted lettering appearing on a black background. Image Operation Study #1 discusses this operation in greater depth.

It is important to realize that contrast enhancement, like any image operation, does not have an absolute "goodness" quality for which we always aim. Different applications see contrast enhancement as meaning different things, depending on what the user wishes to ultimately see in the processed image.

PHOTOMETRIC CORRECTION

In any system of image gathering and display, we encounter certain degradations which are based on the equipment used. These degradations come in the form of photometric and geometric distortions. *Photometric distortions* relate to brightness response incongruencies of a sensor device. *Geometric distortions* are spatially oriented. Ideally, the system should produce an image identical to the original scene with no degradations added. However, using available equipment, some distortions will occur, although they may be slight. Often space flight imaging equipment is purposely not optimized for low distortion due to size and weight considerations. In such a case, the idea is to characterize the degradations before flight and correct them as image data are received on the ground. Spacecraft movement may cause geometric smearing but if the distortion is well characterized, correction is often simple. Geometric corrections will be covered under frame processing.

The word *photometric* refers to the properties of light intensity response. In this case, we are concerned with the intensity response characteristics of a sensor device to illu-

44

mination. Photometric correction, therefore, deals with the correction of sensor illumination response deficiencies. An important word here is correction. This is not an enhancement as previously defined, but a correction based on factual knowledge of the distortion.

Though this process holds true for correcting degradations induced by any photosensor or display device, we will dwell on the spacecraft example. A spacecraft image sensor is generally comprised of a solid-state photosensor device, like a photo-diode, that converts light intensity to a voltage level. The voltage level, in turn, represents a sensed brightness gray level. The device is scanned horizontally, sweeping out lines of image data, while scanning vertically to sweep the entire frame. Of interest to us are the intensity response parameters of the photosensor device—if the light impinging the surface of the device doubles in brightness, does its output voltage level double? A typical photosensor device response may be similar to that seen in Figure 5-5. Using this curve we note nonlinearities where the response deviates from a straight line. To correct this effect, we use a mapping function that counteracts the bad effects by mapping the curved response back to a linear response.

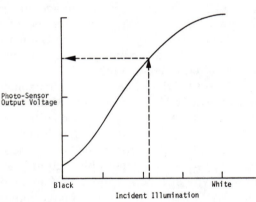

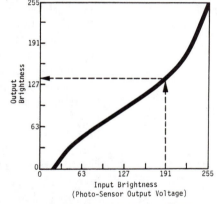

Figure 5-5
(a) Typical photosensor response curve.

(b) Map to correct the photo-sensor response nonlinearities.

We may further extend this operation to correct image data being sent to a display device in order to compensate for display distortions. For instance, a television monitor (or the like) may not produce a brightness on the screen, at any one point, linearly related to the driving voltage representing the point. These degradations, once characterized, may be corrected before sending the image to the monitor much in the same way as sensor correction was done.

ART APPLICATIONS

Today's graphic artist has at hand the power of image processing, with point operations playing a major role. These processes offer the ability to alter gray scale attributes.

Once photographic darkroom techniques, they may now be done quickly, repeatedly, and without chemicals, greatly increasing flexibility. Silkscreen mask generation is one such application.

Silkscreen prints are generally comprised of several colors—say four—all overlaid with one being the background color. To produce the overlay masks, the artist may strip all but the two high-order brightness bits from each pixel's gray level. This leaves a four-gray-level image. Each gray level represents what each overlay will look like. To generate an overlay, one gray level is selected and set to white while all other pixels assume black. By doing this four times, once for each gray level, the overlay masks are generated. Photographing the display monitor each time allows transposition to the silkscreen medium itself. Of course, with simple point processing, an endless variety of other interesting effects are at the hand of the inspired artist.

Pixel Point Processing/Dual Image

We have seen how point operations work on single images; let us now apply this technique to image pairs. Instead of mapping pixel brightness from one image to an output image, we now map two pixel brightnesses, one from each of two input images, into an output image. Again, we are talking with regard to point processes which implies each pixel is handled independently.

The mapping function for dual images becomes somewhat more involved than that of single images. With 8-bit input pixels, each may take on one of 256 different brightnesses. Since each pixel in an input pair is independent, we have a total of 256×256 different possible input combinations being mapped into 256 possible output gray levels. The map for this type of function must be displayed in three dimensions and, unlike the single-image point map, is not easily interpreted. For this reason, we generally work in terms of a *combination function*. This name is appropriate because it refers to the way in which the two input images are combined. Our dual image point process equation is of the form

$$O(x,y) = I_1(x,y) \, \& \, I_2(x,y)$$

where $I_1(x,y)$ and $I_2(x,y)$ represent the two input images. The symbol & is used to denote the combination function. As before, it is implied that all pixels in the images are operated upon.

Combination functions include mathematical and logical operators such as $+$, $-$, $\times$, $/$, AND, OR and EXclusive OR. We now have the ability to add, subtract, multiply, divide, AND, OR, and EXclusive OR image pairs, opening an additional world of point processing. For instance, dual-im-

Figure 5-6
(a) Original image #1.

(b) Original image #2.

(c) Pixel-by-pixel addition of both images.

age addition operations are used for frame averaging in the reduction of random picture noise. Addition may also be used for the simple superimposing of two images; this is depicted in Figure 5-6. Subtraction techniques yield the ability to subtract out consistent background patterns and detect object motion from frame to frame. More on these operations may be found in Image Operation Studies #17, #18 and #19.

Pixel Group Processing

Pixel point processing allowed image gray-scale occupancy modification and image combination, which are both important image processing tools. What point operations did not allow was the spatial modification of scene detail within an image. Everything was handled pixel by pixel, with no interest in adjoining pixels. It turns out that when operating on any one particular pixel, adjoining pixels can give valuable information concerning brightness trends in the area being processed. These brightness trends open doors to the world of *spatial filtering*.

Earlier, the concept of spatial frequency was mentioned. Spatial frequency is the term used to define two-dimensional frequency. An image is said to be composed of many basic frequency subcomponents, ranging from high to low. Where rapid brightness transitions are prevalent, we have high spatial frequency. Slow transitions represent low frequency. Wherever a sharp edge is present—say, a transition from white to black within a one pixel distance—the highest frequencies in the image are found. Making use of this information, we may generate output images showing only the high-frequency or low-frequency components, a class of image processing known as spatial filtering. Additional spatial filtering operations make it possible to generate images that show only where individual sharp transitions occur. These processes ultimately yield image edge detection and enhancement.

In dealing with spatial filtering, we talk about the *spatial convolution* operation. Convolution is a mathematical method used in signal analysis. Although the operation is mathematically complex, we may discuss it in an intuitive, pictorial manner. Spatial convolution is the method we use to calculate what is going on with the pixel brightnesses around the point of processing. As in point processing, we move across the image, pixel-by-pixel, placing a result at the same location in the output image as we are in the input image. It is the calculation that is different. The output pixel brightness becomes dependent on a group of pixels surrounding the pixel in which we are interested. By taking information about the center pixel's neighbors, we are able to calculate spatial frequency activity in the area and therefore are capable of making discretionary decisions regarding the area's spatial frequency content. Let us see how spatial convolution is carried out.

For every pixel in the input image, we calculate a value for the output image pixel by calculating a *weighted average* of it and its surrounding neighbors. The average is formed from a group of pixels, called a *kernel,* around, and including, the center pixel being processed. The dimensions are that of a square. The kernel may have the dimensions 1×1, which is the trivial case giving simply a point operation, 2×2, 3×3, and so on. The operation is said to increase in *degrees of freedom*, the larger the kernel size. This means that the flexibility of the spatial filter is increased by taking into account more neighboring pixels in the calculation. The accepted general-purpose kernel size is 3×3. This is because enough freedom is maintained and yet computation time is minimized.

The term *weighted average* is best described by first considering a conventional nonweighted average. As with any averaging of numbers, we add the numbers together and divide by the number of terms in the average. This gives us a single number based on the information present in all the numbers in the operation. For a 3×3 kernel, we would add the 9 pixel brightnesses together and divide the result by 9. A weighted average, on the other hand, is formed by attaching a multiplicative weighting factor to each term in the average. By altering these weighting factors, or *convolution coefficients,* certain pixels will have more or less influence on the overall average. In fact, correctly selecting the proper weighting coefficients allows us to carry out high and low pass image filters along with a variety of edge enhancement filters.

The mechanics of spatial convolution are fairly straightforward. In carrying out a 3×3 kernel convolution, nine weighting coefficients are defined and labeled *A* through *I*. This array of coefficients is called the *convolution mask.* Every pixel in the image is evaluated with its eight neighbors, using this mask, to produce a resultant pixel value to be placed in the output image. A graphical representation of the operation is shown in Figure 5-7. The mask is placed over each input pixel. The pixel and its eight neighbors are multiplied by their respective weighting coefficients and summed. The result is placed in the output image at the same center pixel location. This operation ocurs for each pixel in the input image; in our case, 256 × 256 = 65,536 times. Each operation requires nine multiplications and nine additions. As we can see, a full image convolution requires on the order of a half-million multiplications and additions—not a quick process. Chapter 7 will show how special-purpose image processing hardware can drastically reduce this computational time.

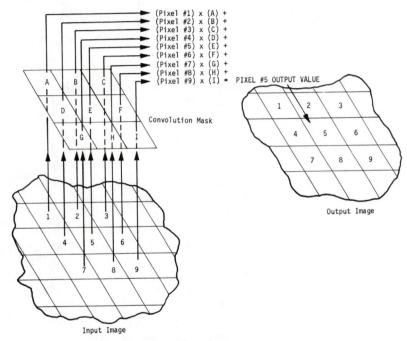

Figure 5-7 Spatial convolution calculation flow for pixel #5.

Research in image processing has yielded a variety of convolution masks for use as standard processing functions. Actually, the masks and the convolution process itself are no more than an application of standard mathematical functions in *linear system theory*. The mathematical foundations of linear system theory may be found in most texts dealing with electrical signal analysis. We will now review commonly used convolution masks and discuss how they work to effect our end goals in image processing.

SPATIAL FILTERING

The term *spatial filtering* implies the separation of frequency components within a two-dimensional base of data, or in our case, an image. The frequency components are spatial frequencies which relate to the rapidity of change in gray levels over a certain spatial distance. Implementing a *high pass filter* will accentuate high-frequency details, leaving low-frequency details attenuated as a result. A *low pass filter* has the inverse effect. Edge enhancement operations are additional spatial filters with special edge detection properties. Since these filters play an important role in edge enhancement, they will be covered separately in the following section.

A spatial low pass filter has the effect of passing, or leaving untouched, low-spatial-frequency components of an image. High-frequency components are attenuated, leaving them virtually absent in the output image. A common low pass convolution mask is comprised of all nine coefficients having the value of 1/9:

1/9   1/9   1/9
1/9   1/9   1/9
1/9   1/9   1/9

Two aspects are immediately evident—the coefficients sum to 1 ($9 \times 1/9 = 1$) and they are all positive numbers. These two facts hold true for all low pass filter masks. Figure 5-8 illustrates a low passed image.

Figure 5-8
(a) Original image.

(b) Low pass filtered image.

To gain an intuitive feeling for how the low pass filter works, we may discuss the convolution output values as the mask is passed over regions of an image having different spatial frequency characteristics. If each pixel in a 3×3 group has the same brightness value, the result will be that of the constant pixel value. This correlates with the fact that there is a spatial frequency of 0 in the neighborhood—no gray level change at all. A frequency of 0 is the lowest possible and, of course, would be expected to be passed by the low pass filter unchanged. If the pixels in a neighborhood change rapidly from white to black every other location, the calculated output pixel value will be that of the average of all nine input values. As the mask moves over all pixels in a high-frequency area, they are replaced by their group averages, producing an output image that removes the high-frequency details. The visual effect is that of blurring. So we see that the output image is related to spatial frequency of the input image, slow-changing areas are left unchanged or changed slightly where fast-changing areas get averaged out to yield only the slow-changing aspects.

If we were to pass the low pass mask over an area with a single pixel width line having a constant background pixel brightness, we would expect the line to be blurred. This is because the line represents a high spatial frequency content. In fact, a sharply defined line actually is composed of frequency components spanning the spectrum of low to high frequencies. As the mask is moved over the line, pixels are replaced by the average of the bright line pixels and the constant background pixels. We expect the resultant value to be somewhere between the two. The line becomes blurred into the background. Only the low-frequency components of the line remain at the end of the entire image convolution. The low pass filter is further discussed in Image Operation Study #6.

The low pass image filter becomes intuitively clear with a little studying. By running the mask over regions of varying details, we see the results corresponding with the passing of low-frequency details and the blocking of high-frequency details. All masks may be analyzed in this same intuitive manner.

Low pass filtering reduces high-frequency detail in an image. The effect is a mellowed, or slightly blurred, image. Low pass filtering allows analysis of low-frequency details of an image without the disruption of high-frequency details. It also plays an important role in the unsharp masking enhancement operation, discussed in Image Operation Study #9.

The high pass filter has basically the opposite effect of the low pass filter. It accentuates high-frequency spatial components while leaving low-frequency components untouched. A common high pass mask is comprised of a 9 in the center location with −1s in the surrounding locations:

$$
\begin{array}{ccc}
-1 & -1 & -1 \\
-1 & 9 & -1 \\
-1 & -1 & -1
\end{array}
$$

We note that the coefficients add to 1 and, furthermore, smaller coefficients surround the large positive center coefficient. A high passed image is illustrated in Figure 5-9.

The fact that the high pass mask contains a large positive coefficient in the center surrounded by smaller coefficients gives us a clue as to its operation. It tells us that the center pixel in the group of input pixels being processed carries a high weight whereas the surrounding ones act to oppose it. If the center pixel possesses a brightness vastly different from its immediate neighbors, the surrounding pixel effect becomes negligible and the output value becomes a brightened version of the original center pixel. The large difference indicates a sharp transition in gray level, and we would expect the high-frequency content transition to be accentuated in the output image. On the other hand, if the surrounding pixel brightnesses are large enough to counteract the center pixel's weight, the ultimate result is based more on an average of all pixels involved.

It may be interesting to note that if all pixels in a 3 × 3 group are equal, the result is simply the same value. This is equivalent to the low pass filter's response over constant regions. What this means is that this high pass filter does not attenuate low-frequency spatial components. Rather, it emphasizes high-frequency components while leaving low-frequency components untouched.

Figure 5-9
(a) Original image.

(b) High pass filtered image.

High pass filtering of an image adds accentuation to the edges, or transition areas, within it. This effect often gives the viewer a more pleasing image. Additionally, details muted by the background and low-frequency noise become apparent where they may have been barely visible in the original. Both high and low pass filter functions also fill important roles when used in conjunction with point processes. More on the high pass filter may be found in Image Operation Study #7.

EDGE DETECTION/ENHANCEMENT

Enhancement of edges in an image is an operation used in feature extraction, an important class of image processing. The operation basically reduces an image to display only its edge information. This information is then used for feature, or object, recognition by high-level algorithms. Additionally, a useful enhancement operation is carried out by adding the edge enhanced image back to the original using a dual image point process. The result is a crisper image displaying sharper edge detail.

Edge enhancements may be implemented through spatial filtering. Three particularly useful filters are found to be quite common in many image processing tasks. They are known as *shift and difference, gradient* and *Laplacian*. All three enhancements are based on the slope of pixel brightness occurring within a pixel group. To further define the term *slope* in an image context, think of the brightness of each pixel as being represented by a height coming out from the page toward the observer (see Figure 5-10). We see an image mound rather than the standard gray tone representation; the brighter the pixel, the higher the mound. By measuring the slope of the mound within any given pixel group, we have a value for how steep the incline is. A large value corresponds to a steep slope and means a large change in gray level. A small value indicates small slope which is equivalent to a small change in gray level. Since edges are, by definition, sharp brightness changes, large slopes indicate the presence of an edge.

The simplest edge enhancement operation is the shift and difference method. This procedure allows us to extract horizontal and vertical edge information. By shifting an image to the left by one pixel and then subtracting it from the original, vertical edges become apparent. On a pixel-by-pixel basis, we subtract the horizontal neighbor, giving a value of their brightness difference, or slope. Of course, a large difference is yielded by two adjacent pixels of greatly varying brightnesses. The result is an image appearing as an embossing (see Figure 5-11).

The analogous horizontal edge enhancement is implemented by shifting the image upward by one pixel and carrying out the subtraction. Since the success of all enhancements is evaluated subjectively, this edge enhance-

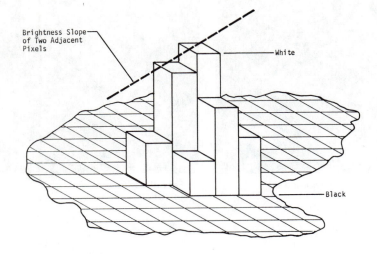

Brightness Slope of Two Adjacent Pixels

White

Black

Figure 5-10 Pixel brightness represented by height, illustrating the concept of brightness slope.

ment technique often proves valuable. The shift and difference operation may be carried out using a dual image subtraction process or a group process. Image Operation Study #10 discusses this operation in more depth.

The gradient operation forms a directional edge enhancement. Using a 3×3 kernel, eight gradient images may be generated from an original. Each highlights edges oriented in one of the eight compass directions—N, NE, E, SE, S, SW, W, and NW. Figure 5-11 illustrates an East directional gradient. The mask oriented for the East direction is given.

−1	1	1
−1	−2	1
−1	1	1

Note that the coefficients add to 0. This means that as the mask passes over a region of the image having a constant brightness, a result of 0 is produced. Of course, this represents a brightness slope of 0, which is exactly what a region of constant brightness has.

Using the East mask, a transition from dark to light, going left to right, will be accentuated. This is because a positive East brightness slope exists. Brightness slopes in other directions sum to a negative value, which is forced to 0, or black. The response of the gradient operation for a one-dimensional edge is seen in Figure 5-12. Where the gradient generates negative results, the output value is set to 0, since negative brightnesses are undefined. The gradient image appears black wherever the original image brightnesses are constant. Edges with the correct directional orientation in the original image are seen as white. Additional discussion of the gradient operation along with masks for all eight directional enhancements may be found in Image Operation Study #11.

53

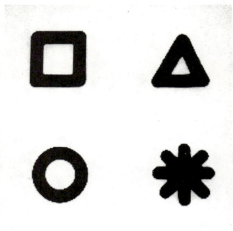

Figure 5-11
(a) Original pattern image.

(b) Vertical shift and difference edge enhancement.

(c) East direction gradient edge enhancement.

(f) Original image of bridge.

(g) Vertical shift and difference edge enhancement.

(h) East direction gradient edge enhancement.

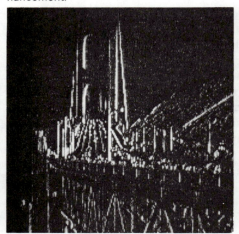

The Laplacian edge enhancement is an omnidirectional operation, highlighting all edges regardless of their orientation. This operation is based on the rate of change of the brightness slope within a 3 × 3 pixel group. The common Laplacian mask is comprised of an 8 in the center location with −1s in the surrounding locations.

$$\begin{array}{ccc} -1 & -1 & -1 \\ -1 & 8 & -1 \\ -1 & -1 & -1 \end{array}$$

The coefficients add to 0 and, as in the high pass filter mask, negative valued coefficients surround the large positive center coefficient. Figure 5-11 illustrates a Laplacian edge enhanced image.

The Laplacian enhancement generates sharper peaks at edges than does the gradient operation. Any brightness slope, whether positive or negative, is accentuated, giving

Laplacian edge enhancement.

(e) Horizontal line detect.

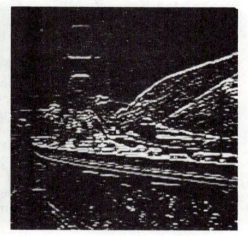

Laplacian edge enhancement.

(j) Horizontal line detect.

the Laplacian its omnidirectional quality. In the human visual system, the eye-brain system applies a Laplacian-like enhancement to everything we view. Because of this, a natural sharpening of images may be achieved by adding a brightness scaled Laplacian enhanced image to the original. The results of this procedure often produce a natural-looking sharpened image with subjectively pleasing qualities.

The Laplacian image appears black wherever the original brightnesses are constant or linearly changing. Edges made of nonlinear brightness transitions are highlighted as white. The Laplacian operation is discussed in additional depth in Image Operation Study #12.

The above methods for edge enhancements play a major role in machine vision. Whether the application is automated assembly-line material inspection or feature recognition, these processes are the first used to condition the raw images. Before a computer can actually attempt a

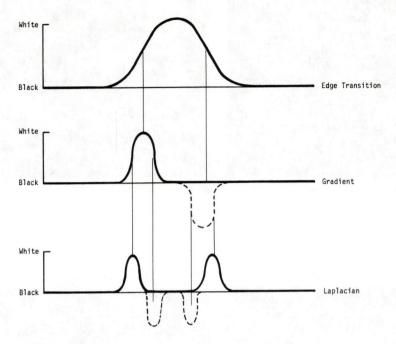

Figure 5-12 Response characteristics of the gradient and Laplacian edge enhancement operations.

recognition process, though, the image must generally be further processed. One such operation is the binary contrast enhancement, discussed earlier. Another operation often found useful is a *line segment enhancement*. A line enhancement operation emphasizes line segments within the image.

Figure 5-11 on pp. 54–55 illustrates an image processed by the horizontal line segment enhancement operation. The mask for this operation is given.

$$
\begin{array}{ccc}
-1 & -1 & -1 \\
2 & 2 & 2 \\
-1 & -1 & -1
\end{array}
$$

Again, the coefficients add to 0. This tells us that constant brightness regions of the original image will become black when processed. Only line segments are left highlighted.

In factory process control applications, binary contrast enhancement is often evoked following the line segment enhancement. The ultimate result is an image more intelligible to computer object-recognition algorithms. More on line segment enhancement operations is found in Image Operation Study #13.

We have covered a section of image processing dealing with the enhancement of images based on brightness trend information within a 3×3 pixel group. Masks for these processes may be altered or entirely redefined to effect the user's end result. Especially powerful is the combination of point processing with group processing. The operations covered represent the most-used functions and serve as an introduction to the inner workings of group processing.

56

Frame Processing

Frame processing is the term given to the collection of image processing operations that do not fall within the confines of point or group processing. Frame processes encompass a wide variety of algorithms, each as different from another as point processes were from group processes. Because of this diversity, processing hardware within an image processing system rarely includes the capability of handling some, if any, frame processes. Instead the job is usually left to the host computer to be carried out in software. The actual processing implementation of these processes will be discussed in Chapter 7.

As would be expected, all image analysis and coding operations fall under the category of frame processing. Neither of these classes of image processing operations may be handled by the point or group processes. A common example of image analysis frame processing is that of the histogram, discussed in Chapter 4.

Frame processes are often time consuming, yet serve as useful and necessary functions for a variety of image processing applications. Three commonly used operations are overviewed here—geometric operations, image transforms, and data compression. Additionally, an operation known as the median filter is discussed in Image Operation Study #8.

GEOMETRIC OPERATIONS

Geometric operations, as applied to images, provide for the spatial reorientation of pixel data within an image scene. Pixel data from an input image may be transformed into new spatial locations, as defined by a geometric algorithm, producing a resulting image of altered characteristics. Geometric operations are often employed in image processing as a primary or ancillary function to processes from the point or group classes.

Three basic geometric processes allow for the sizing, orientation, and movement of images. They are image scaling, rotation, and translation. These operations permit the user to do simple pixel spatial transformation.

All geometric operations are performed by moving pixels from their original spatial coordinates in the input image to new coordinates in the output image. The general equation for these operations is

$$I(x,y) \rightarrow O(x',y')$$

where (x',y') are the transformed coordinates of the pixel brightness originally located at coordinates (x,y). Each geometric operation is, therefore, defined by a coordinate transform equation that defines the new x' and y' output coordinates for an input pixel at (x,y).

Image scaling deals with the enlarging and shrinking of an image or portion of an image. The general coordinate

57

transform equations for this function is given by the equations

$$x' = Sx \text{ and}$$
$$y' = Sy$$

where x and y are the coordinates of the input pixel being processed, x' and y' are the new output pixel coordinates and S is the scaling factor. S acts to modify the coordinates of the pixel brightness at (x,y) rather than the pixel brightness itself, as did the mapping function, M, in point processing. The scaling factor dictates the amount of magnification or demagnification to occur. For example, $S = 2$ represents a magnification of 2, where $S = 1/2$ would be a magnification of 1/2, or a shrinkage by a factor of 2. Figure 5-13 illustrates image magnification and shrinkage.

To see how the formula works, let us follow it through for a magnification of 2 applied to a 256 × 256 image. A pixel is retrieved from the input image at coordinates (x,y)—say location (67,67). The scaling factor acts to multiply both x and y by 2, yielding $(x'y')$ equal to (134,134). The original pixel brightness taken from location (67,67) in the input image is, therefore, placed at location (134,134) in the output image. Continuing the process across the input image line, we ultimately arrive at the pixel residing at (127,67). Applying the scaling factor, S, to the coordinates gives (254,134) as the new output coordinates. Incrementing to the next input pixel, (128,67), the scaling will yield output coordinates of (256,67)—out of range for a 256 × 256 output image. The processing of line 67 is complete. The pixel coordinates in line 67 have been expanded from between 0 through 127 to 0 through 254, a magnification of two. The analogous process happens on a line-by-line basis. In all, the pixel coordinates from pixel (0,0) to (127,127) are mapped to form a new output image filling the entire 256 × 256 image frame.

The obvious question is what happens to the odd lines and pixel locations in the output image, since nothing is directly mapped into them? Since we have effectively mapped a 128 × 128 image into a 256 × 256 image, there is no valid pixel information to be placed in the odd locations. To make the output image more appealing, however, the pixel to the immediate left is usually replicated into the odd pixel location. Likewise, the line of pixels above an odd line is replicated into the odd line below. The reduction in spatial resolution is the natural artifact of doing a magnification. In each axis, we have expanded half the pixel data into a full frame.

Image shrinking follows the same principles as magnification. In a shrinking by a factor of $2(S = 1/2)$, the input image of size 256 × 256 will be mapped into an output image of size 128 × 128.

Figure 5-13
(a) Image magnification by factor of 2.

(b) Image shrinkage by factor of 2.

Scaling serves a variety of purposes in image processing. It may be used to simply crop a scene before further processing is evoked. For image composition, it allows several input images to be size adjusted before they are assembled into a final output image collage using a dual image point process image addition. Also, image registration between two input images in a dual point process may utilize the scaling operation. Image scaling is discussed further in Image Operation Study #14.

Image rotation provides the user with the ability to rotate images about a center point. The coordinate transform equations are

$x' = x\cos\theta + y\sin\theta$ and
$y' = -x\sin\theta + y\cos\theta$

where x and y are the input image pixel coordinates, x' and y' are the new output pixel location, (x',y'), and θ represents the angle of clockwise rotation of the image about the image center point. A θ of angle 0 to 360 degrees may be specified, allowing the rotation of an image through any required angle. Figure 5-14 illustrates an image rotated through an angle of 330°.

The mathematics behind the rotation algorithm is an application of basic trigonometry. The derivation of the equations may be found in almost any text dealing with the subject. The center point of rotation is the center of the image and must therefore be defined as the pixel coordinate origin for this operation. Pixels then have the coordinates −127 to 128, going across the image from left to right. Likewise, lines from top to bottom have the coordinates −127 to 128. For the sake of following the process through, we will use the simple example of $\theta = 90°$. We calculate $\sin 90° = 1$ and $\cos 90° = 0$. The equations boil down to $x' = y$ and $y' = -x$. So plugging in the input pixel coordinates of (127,67), for example, yields the resulting output image coordinates of (67,−177). Applying the spatial transformation to all pixels within the input image will yield an output image rotated by 90°.

A concern in image rotation comes up when rotating an image by an angle that is not a multiple of 90°. As we saw in the example, the 90° rotation maps pixels one for one from the input to output image. This also holds true for 180° and 270° rotations for the $\sin\theta$ and $\cos\theta$ terms will be either 1 or 0. When rotating through an angle that is not a multiple of 90°, however, we have $\sin\theta$ and $\cos\theta$ terms that are fractional. As a result, the calculated output pixel coordinates rarely are integer numbers. So where does the pixel brightness go if (x',y') are not integer numbers? There are two ways to handle the problem. One is to place the pixel brightness at the nearest pixel location. This technique tends to turn straight lines into jagged lines when rotated, sometimes causing results disturbing to the viewer.

Figure 5-14 330° Image rotation.

A second technique is called interpolation. A pixel falling between locations in the output image will always be somewhere in between four valid pixel locations. One form of interpolation divides the total pixel brightness into parts to be placed at the four valid pixel locations. The brightness division is determined by the distance that the transformed input pixel falls from each of the four output pixel locations. Since other pixels are also mapped to fractional pixel locations in the output image, there may be up to four input pixels contributing some brightness to any one output pixel location. Figure 5-15 shows this interpolation scheme.

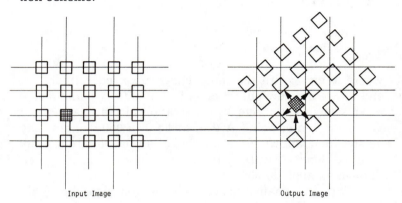

Input Image   Output Image

Figure 5-15 Pixel location interpolation.

Image rotation is used for many of the same reasons as scaling. The user is simply allowed an additional method of geometric manipulation for whatever reason may be appropriate. Image Operation Study #15 further discusses geometric rotation.

The last basic geometric operation is that of *image translation*, allowing the up-and-down, side-to-side movement of an image. The coordinate transform equations for image translation are given by the equations

$x' = x + T_x$ and
$y' = y + T_y$

where x and y comprise the input pixel coordinates, x' and y' form the output coordinates and T_x with T_y define the translation in the x and y directions. An input pixel is shifted side to side by the number of pixels indicated by T_x while the shift up and down is specified by T_y, thereby effecting the translation. All the input pixel coordinates are shifted by the amounts given by T_x and T_y.

For example, with $T_x = 10$ and $T_y = -20$, an input pixel at location (127,67) will be mapped to the location (127−20, 67+10), or (107,77), in the output image. When applied to all pixels in the input image, the net result will be an image moved to the right 10 pixels and up 20 pixels. Figure 5-16 shows a typical image translation.

Translation may be combined with scaling and rotation, netting the user the capability of total geometric image manipulation. This kind of image manipulation is useful in corrective geometric processing of many image scenes as a prelude to other operations. See Image Operation Study #16 for more on image translation.

A type of geometric transformation commonly used to correct spatially distorted images is known as *rubber sheet transformation*. This process may be thought of as working with an input image printed on a sheet of rubber. The rubber is then stretched and pinned down at selected points so that the original image is geometrically contorted to effect a desired end result. This type of geometric correction finds a variety of uses, for instance, spatial correction for an image sensor, an operation parallel to photometric correction.

In an image sensor, there often exists some sort of spatial nonlinearity. This type of distortion is manifested as spatial bulges or contractions acting to distort the sensed image. These nonlinearities are usually slight and cause no problem to the user of the images. However, in certain applications—spaceborne imaging, for instance—weight and size constraints may force the design of an image sensor to be less than perfect. In these cases, the use of a rubber sheet transformation may be needed.

The basic approach to implementing a rubber sheet transformation is to define the mapping of input pixel locations to output pixel locations. This can be done with a massive spatial look-up table directly mapping input pixels into their new output locations. Implementing such a process can be very time consuming. Instead, we use a more general approach, still retaining a large degree of freedom in the definition of the transformation. Taking the rubber sheet image, we envision what areas of the image are to be stretched and to what degree. The stretching is then thought of as being carried out by pinning points of the sheet down. These points are called *control points.* By mathematically defining where the control points are located and what degree of stretching is to occur between them, we are able to calculate the input-to-output pixel transformation. Interpolation, as seen before, must also be used since the mapping will generally not be one to one.

The rubber sheet transformation idea may be extended to include the correction of viewing geometry problems and some sensor movement induced problems. Say, for example, an image is taken of the flat surface of an object at a perspective other than perpendicular to the surface plane. The resulting image is distorted in that square coordinate points on the surface appear quadrilateral in the image. By mapping the points of the imaged quadrilateral area into a square, we may recover the view of the area as it would have appeared in a perpendicular imaging ar-

Figure 5-16 Image translation —64 pixels up, 50 pixels to right.

61

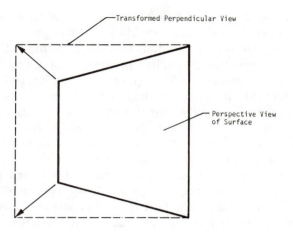

Figure 5-17 Rubber sheet transformation of quadrilateral area to square area.

rangement. Figure 5-17 illustrates this transformation. Likewise, mapping into another desired perspective angle is possible. Getting more involved is the perspective alteration necessary in correcting an image of a planetary object. In this case, the spherical curvature of the imaged surface must also be accounted for.

Some image sensor movement problems, as encountered in spacecraft, may also be handled by a rubber sheet transformation. In an imaging device that has a line of light sensors—common in Earth mapping satellites—we may experience sensor movement during the accumulation of enough lines to compose an entire image frame. This effect may, in some cases, yield an image of rectangular dimensions where the actual object area covered was square. We may use rubber sheet transformation to stretch out the shorter dimension of the rectangle and derive the original geometry of the object. Adding in movement that is not along the imaging axis adds to the complexity of this process.

All of the rubber sheet corrections reduce to straightforward mathematical models as long as the geometric distortion is precisely defined before processing commences. In the sensor spatial nonlinearity correction, the distortion may be characterized by imaging a square grid and deriving the proper equations to map whatever the sensor output image is into the original square grid pattern. From that point on, the geometric correction map will remain the same regardless of what is imaged. Likewise, as long as a spacecraft's movement is well defined and viewing perspective is known, the associated corrections pose no major difficulty.

We have discussed a variety of geometric corrections available to the user as needed. By picking and choosing the appropriate process or combination of processes, we have the flexibility to enhance geometrically poor images, making them more useful than they were in their original form.

TRANSFORMS

The discussion on spatial frequency content of an image allowed us to see that a scene is composed of varying spatial frequency components. Group processing operations then provided the ability to accentuate or attenuate certain frequency components of the image, depending on the coefficients used in the convolution mask—for instance, high and low pass filtering. Very powerful operations, known as *frequency transforms* can be used to give a pictorial view of the spatial frequency component breakdown of an image. Additionally, these transforms may aid in the specific filtering of undesired components.

An image scene is composed of two-dimensional spatial frequency components. These frequencies have varying orientation—horizontal, vertical, etc.—and are defined as having an amplitude and phase. It may be further stated that an image may be broken into these frequency components and then reconstructed from their subsequent summation.

A frequency transform gives us the ability to transform an image from the spatial domain to the spatial frequency domain and back again. Applying a frequency transform to an image yields a new image displaying the array of spatial frequencies, and their amplitudes and phases, present in the original image. The frequency image displays the presence of frequency components in an original image by the brightness of points at respective locations. Horizontal frequency is defined along the x-axis and vertical frequency along the y-axis. The brightness of a point in the image corresponds to the amplitude of the frequency component represented by the point's coordinates. Using this frequency domain image, we may easily analyze the spatial frequency content of an image.

Image filtering may be carried out in the frequency domain in a more intuitively straightforward manner than convolution in the spatial domain. To remove a particular frequency band from an image, we may simply set the corresponding area of that frequency image to zero, which removes those frequency components, and transform the frequency image back to the spatial domain. The drawback is in the two transforms that must be executed. Not only are these operations extremely computationally intensive in a time sense, but the cumulative mathematical errors can sometimes lead to problems.

The execution of a low pass filter on an image using the frequency transform method rather than spatial convolution proceeds as follows. A frequency transform is performed on the input image, yielding a spatial frequency image. The frequency image is then multiplied by a frequency mask image where the desired low-frequency components are equal to 1 and all others to 0. The resulting image is identical to the original frequency image in the low-frequency region, but zero elsewhere; there are no longer any high-frequency components in the frequency image. This image is then inverse frequency transformed back to the spatial domain where we are left with a low passed version of the original image. High pass filtering is handled similarly by multiplying the frequency image by a mask image with the desired high-frequency regions equal to 1 and the low regions to 0. Of course, the frequency mask image may take on values other than just 0 and 1. By selecting appropriate numbers, the degree of frequency accentuation and attenuation may be controlled.

A great power of frequency transform filtering is the ability to do highly selective frequency filtering. For example, an image with a periodic noise, appearing as bands across the image, will have a frequency image with bright spots at the locations in the frequency domain where the noise frequency exists. By multiplying the frequency image by a mask that "zeros" the bright spot (thereby performing a band rejection filter at that frequency), the resulting spatial domain image will be devoid of the noise bands. An artifact of the filtration will be that any good image data comprised of the filtered spatial frequency will also be lost. However, the narrow frequency filtering allowed by the transform method will produce minimal disturbance to the rest of the image.

Frequency transforms come in a variety of forms. The distinguishing differences are the conventions used in which spatial frequencies are broken down into components. Although the exact transform type to be used is dependent on the application, the most common ones encountered are the Fourier, Hadamard, and Haar transforms. Derivations and applicability of these and other transforms may be found in texts dealing with signal processing and analysis.

Frequency transforms as applied to image processing can prove to be useful and sometimes invaluable tools. They are also time consuming, computationally intensive operations, generally leading to expensive implementation. Transforms are rarely supported on board image processing systems; they are most often handled by a host computer with fast numerical computation capabilities.

DATA COMPRESSION

Images of even moderate size are comprised of large amounts of data. Because of the ever-increasing desire to transmit and store images, it is common to code the data into a form less space consuming, thereby allowing speedier transmission or denser storage. There are numerous techniques currently employed to handle this type of coding, some more useful than others, depending on the application. Image data compression falls in the important class of image coding operations.

In an image of a natural scene, there will tend to be redundant information. When properly processed, this information may be reduced to a simpler form, producing an image requiring less data needed to describe it. To see this, we examine an image (such as Figure 3–3) from left to right along a single line. Gray levels go up and down. Except for areas composed of high spatial frequencies, these levels tend to change slowly or even remain constant over substantial lengths. Often, the majority of a line may be the same gray level. Using this knowledge, we may employ techniques of image coding that can be quite effective in the reduction of data necessary to reconstruct an original image. Two such methods in common use serve as good, easy-to-understand introductions to the area of image data compression. They are *run-length coding* and *differential pulse code modulation,* or DPCM.

Run-length coding may be implemented in a variety of ways; we will look at one method. On a line-by-line basis, we start at the beginning of a line. The brightness of the first pixel is noted. Traveling across the line, we count the number of subsequent pixels of the same brightness. When a different brightness is encountered, we place in the coded image file the constant brightness of the first group of pixels and how many there were. The process then repeats itself. For instance, if there were 53 pixels of the same brightness in the first group, they will be coded into two 8-bit binary numbers. The first number represents the brightness and the second represents the number of pixels in the length. The 53 8-bit pixels have been coded into two 8-bit numbers, a substantial data reduction.

Of course, if the brightness of pixels is changing every pixel location across the line, the run-length method will require twice the data storage of the original image itself. Remember, each time a brightness change is encountered, two 8-bit numbers are required to characterize the previous group of constant pixels, even if that group is only one pixel long. Modifications to the run-length algorithm may further enchance its characteristics, making it more efficient in high spatial frequency areas of an image.

A second coding method of interest is differential pulse code modulation, or DPCM. Instead of working with the principle that there will be long lengths of constant pixels, we assume that any adjacent pixel will tend to be near in brightness to its horizontal neighbor. As we travel across the line, the coded image file is loaded with the difference in brightness from one pixel to the next. Assuming that this change is never to be more than, say, eight gray levels, the coded change value need only be three bits long. Instead of storing the absolute brightness value of all pixels in an image, we simply store the change in brightness as we go from one pixel to the next. For 8-bit pixels; this technique represents an across the board data reduction of $(8 - 3)/8 = 63\%$.

An artifact of this coding technique shows up when the change in brightness from one pixel to the next is larger than eight gray levels. The DPCM method may require several pixel distances to settle in on the correct pixel brightness value after encountering a sharp change. The effect of this phenomenon manifests itself as an apparent horizontal low pass filtering of the image. By increasing the number of bits used to describe the pixel-to-pixel difference, this effect may be minimized. However, the improvement comes at the cost of data reduction efficiency.

Image coding techniques are far ranging. Often the algorithm to be used will be dependent on the type of images to be coded. For instance, both of the above methods work well except when dealing with images comprised largely of high-frequency components.

Implementation of image coding may often be handled in hardware as a final step in some sort of processing before the image is to be transmitted or stored. For general-purpose processors, however, the task is left to the host computer to be carried out in software.

PROCESSING HARDWARE ||||||||

Image Data Handling 6

Commercial image processing equipment is available in a variety of forms. Spanning a broad price range, these systems provide the user with everything from simple image manipulation capabilities to massive, high-volume processing power. One rule of thumb holds when speaking of general-purpose image processing systems—the more a system costs, the faster and more flexible it will be in the processing and handling of image data.

Within any image processing system, regardless of size, there exists the need to support five primary functions of data handling: (1) *image digitization*—the conversion of a video camera input to digital form; (2) *image storage*—the storage of digital image information in memory; (3) *image display*—the conversion of digital image data, residing in image memory, to a television monitor output; (4) *external host computer interface*—the interconnection of the system to a host computer, allowing the reading and writing of image memory for processing, loading and downloading of image data; and (5) *internal image processor interface*—the interconnection of image memory to an internal image processor, allowing the high speed processing of image data. Figure 6-1 illustrates the basic image processing system block diagram.

We will discuss these basic elements of image data handling from an electrical hardware standpoint, dealing

69

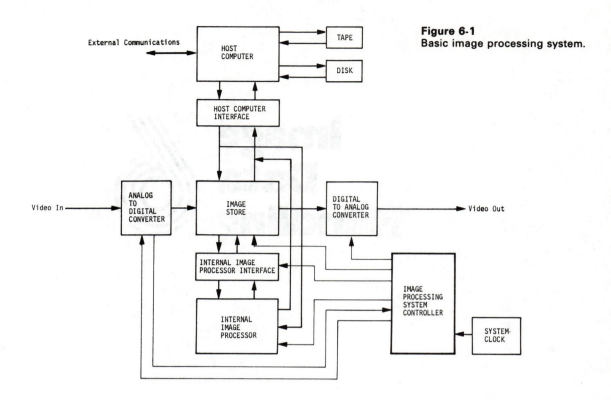

Figure 6-1
Basic image processing system.

with design concepts and methodologies. In particular, emphasis is given to the low-cost system supporting most of the processing power and features of larger systems. Chapter 7 then continues with the hardware design concepts involved in the actual processing of image data.

Image Digitization and Display

A digital system dealing with the processing and handling of picture information requires subsystems to acquire and display the data. These subcomponents of the overall system generally allow standard video signals to be used for input and output. Since standard video is analog in nature, it is necessary to convert the incoming signal to a digital form and the outgoing signal back to an analog form. This is accomplished through the use of analog-to-digital and digital-to-analog converters. These two functions allow digital handling and processing of image data within the processing system which, of course, is what digital image processing is all about.

Video signals to or from various devices such as cameras, video tape recorders, or monitors all fit the specifications of a standard video format. It is this format that the image processor must be able to accept and generate in order to fit within the video equipment domain.

STANDARD TELEVISION VIDEO FORMAT

What we call *standard video format* is the specification of how the video signal looks in an electrical sense. In the case of a video camera, light impinges the surface of an

70

image sensing device, such as a vidicon, and an electrical voltage level corresponding to the amount of light hitting a particular spatial region of the surface is generated. This information is then placed into the standard format and sequenced out of the camera. Along with actual light intensity information, synchronization pulses are added to allow the receiving device—a television monitor, for instance—to identify where the sequence is in the frame data.

A standard video format image is read out on a line-by-line basis from left to right, top to bottom. Additionally, a technique known as *interlacing* is employed. Interlacing refers to the reading of all even-numbered lines, top to bottom, followed by all odd lines. Figure 6-2 shows this sequence of video information. Because of interlacing, the television picture frame is divided into even and odd *fields* composed of the even-numbered lines and odd-numbered lines, respectively. Interlacing is used to produce an apparent update of the entire frame in half the time that a full update actually occurs. The eye's integration of sequential fields gives the impression that the frame is updated twice as often as it really is. This results in a television monitor image with less apparent flicker.

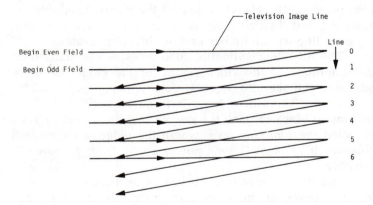

Figure 6-2 The standard television interlace format.

The original black-and-white, or *monochrome*, television format specification is the EIA RS-170 specification produced by the Electronic Industries Association in the late 1950s. It prescribes all timing and voltage level requirements for standard commercial video signals.

A video signal comprises a series of analog television lines. Each line is separated from the next by a synchronization pulse called *horizontal sync*. Furthermore, the fields of the picture frame are separated by a longer synchronization pulse, called *vertical sync*. In the case of a monitor receiving the signal, its electron beam scans the face of the display tube, with the brightness of the beam controlled by the amplitude of the video signal. Whenever a horizontal sync is detected, the beam is reset to the left-most side of the screen and moved down to the next line location. A vertical sync pulse, indicated by a sync pulse of longer duration, resets the beam to the top, left-most point of the screen to a line centered between the first two lines of the previous scan. This allows the current field to be displayed between the previous one.

An entire video frame is made up of 525 lines and is sequenced out every 1/30 of a second or 33.33 milliseconds (mS). This means that each field contains 262 1/2 lines and takes 16.67mS to go out to the monitor. Dividing the number of lines in a field by its time gives the time per line—16.67mS/262.5 = 63.49 microseconds (μS). The reciprocal of this time is 15750 Hz, the television line-scan frequency standard. The determination of line time plays an important role when digitizing, for we must know how fast to sample and digitize the analog video signal to yield the desired number of pixels per line in our subsequent digital image.

Figure 6-3 illustrates the timing and amplitude levels dictated by the RS-170 spec. The vertical sync interval of the signal occurs over the period of the first nine line times having a duration of 571μS. Following the vertical sync period are eleven no-video lines followed by 242 1/2 active video lines. The total 262 1/2 line times compose one entire field. Within each line exists a horizontal sync interval, 10.9μS in duration. This leaves 52.59μS of *active line time* in which the visual portion of the video signal lies. By sampling and digitizing pixels within this active time during each line we obtain our end product digital image.

The RS-170 specification also gives us information on the amplitude of the video signal for the video and sync portions. The overall range is 1 volt swinging from −0.286v to +0.714v. The video swing is from +0.143v to +0.714v relating to black through the grays to white, repectively. 0v is called the *blanking level* where the video is considered "blacker than black." Sync pulses swing from 0v down to −0.286v.

The RS-170 specification has been used as the basis for most monochrome video equipment. Using the specification, we see that the vertical spatial resolution is limited by the number of active lines—242 1/2 per field, or 485 per frame. In the horizontal mode, where the video is a varying analog voltage, it is generally accepted that roughly the equivalent of 380 pixels' worth of image information exists. Of course, enhancement of the various analog circuitry—as in a camera—allow this resolution to increase, making the horizontal resolution as good as the rate of sampling when digitization occurs. The frame rate is given as 33.33mS. This means that the video frame of 485 lines is updated once every 33.33mS.

The accuracy to which the analog voltage amplitude represents a brightness along the horizontal line dictates the brightness resolution contained in the RS-170 video signal. Usually, this resolution is equivalent to roughly seven or eight bits when quantized. Again, enhancement of the analog circuitry in the video equipment can allow greatly increased brightness resolutions to be achieved if required by a particular image processing application.

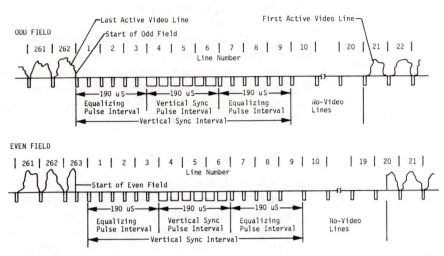

Figure 6-3
(a) RS-170 television timing specification—vertical frame timing.

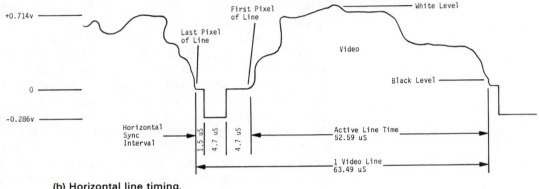

(b) Horizontal line timing.

Other specifications have been written and adopted for use in video systems. The RS-343 specification again deals with monochrome systems but with vertical resolutions between 675 and 1023 lines. The tighter tolerances and modified timing waveforms allow better control when high-resolution systems are implemented. The standard specification for color signals is known as *NTSC* for the originating organization, National Television System Committee. The NTSC specification modifies RS-170 to work with color signals by adding color information to the present signal containing only brightness information.

Many systems, when dealing with color images, simply use three RS-170 type signals, one for each of the three additive primary colors—red, green, and blue. These systems are said to accept and generate *RGB* compatible video. This is the favored technique due to certain color distortions that are manifest in the NTSC conversion. Since color systems generally operate in the RGB mode, they may be thought of as no different than three monochrome systems with the red, green, and blue images being displayed simultaneously. All image processing algorithms work the same, but must be applied independently, to all three images.

73

Now that we have a feeling for what the video input and output of an image processing system looks like, we may explore the digitization and subsequent reconstruction of the information. At that point, we may begin processing images in the digital domain using the techniques covered in Part II of this book.

SAMPLING FOR DIGITIZATION

In Part II, we discussed the fundamentals of sampling an analog signal. Now we must decide just how often to sample the active video line so that the resulting digital image is composed of the desired number of image lines, each subdivided into pixels. As each sample time occurs, a new pixel is derived. The video signal amplitude is converted to a binary number by an analog to digital, or A/D converter. It is this repetitive process that formulates the digital image in its entirety.

The visible portion of a line of video was calculated earlier to take $52.59\mu S$. It is this length of time that will ultimately be chopped into individual discrete pixels. Along with the specifications covered earlier, the RS-170 specification furthermore dictates the dimensions of the television frame to have an *aspect ratio* of 4:3. This means that the horizontal length of the frame is 4/3 the vertical height. This is seen by looking at the face of most any commercially available television. Therefore, the $52.59\mu S$ of active line time represents a longer horizontal distance than the vertical distance spanning the top to bottom of the frame. If we were interested in digitizing a frame to 256 lines $\times$ 256 pixels and were to then pick a sample time of the active line time divided by 256, we would be yielded a digital image 256 $\times$ 256 but with 4/3 more length in the horizontal direction than the vertical. This produces what is called *non-square pixels,* where the actual spatial dimensions of each pixel will be 4/3 units in the horizontal direction and 1 unit in the vertical. Several image processing operations developed for use on "square" pixels, such as the previously defined group processes, cannot tolerate this phenomenon.

To make things more straightforward, image processing systems often work with images with a 1:1 aspect ratio. To obtain a 1:1 aspect ratio in sampling an RS-170 video signal, we must divide the active line time by 4/3, yielding a new active time of $39.44\mu S$. This new horizontal active time is then centered in the once 4:3 screen size by delaying sampling at the beginning of the line by $6.575\mu S$ and leaving $6.575\mu S$ after sampling. The ultimate image will be 1:1 appearing with black on either side to fill the entire 4:3 screen. This square format image will be the basis of all further development (see Figure 6-4).

The first step in the design of an image processor is to define the spatial resolution of the system. This parame-

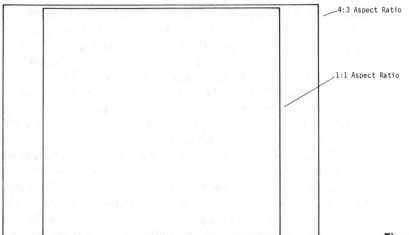

Figure 6-4 4:3 versus 1:1 image aspect ratio.

ter is a variable chosen to fit the particular application that the system is to be suited for. The resolution, as discussed in Chapter 3, may be specified to any dimension—for instance, 64 lines by 64 pixels, 128 × 128, 256 × 256, 512 × 512, etc.—and is generally a power of two, simplifying circuit implementation and computer interface. Certain applications will demand high resolution, and some will not. Typical resolutions found in general image processing systems include 256 × 256 and 512 × 512. Adherence to the tolerances of standard television along with good picture quality make these selections most reasonable. Of course, based on the application, systems of higher resolution are readily available. For the purposes of the following discussions, we will discuss hardware dealing with 256 × 256 and 512 × 512 resolutions.

Using the RS-170 specification, we have seen the television image frame to be divided into two fields, each consisting of 242 1/2 lines. Let us discard the half line and assume the field to be composed of 242 lines. We now have the option of digitizing a single field of 242 lines or both fields of 484 lines. When we speak of a 256-line digital image, what we often actually have is only 242 visual lines of information. Similarly, a 512-line resolution refers to 484 active lines. Since we are working in the digital domain, the numbers 256 and 512 are the closest powers of two to the actual lines available for digitizing and, therefore, are used in the further design of all sequencing logic and memory architecture.

In a 256-line image system, the lines of one field are digitized and stored in memory while the other field is ignored. The displayed image will appear as having half the line resolution of a standard television image. The 512-line case calls for digitizing both fields, yielding the full standard television resolution.

Individual pixels of the digitized image are acquired by sampling the active portion of the video line at equal time intervals. We calculated earlier that the active line time for a 1:1 image was 39.44μS. Within this time, either 256 or 512 samples must be taken, converted through an A/D converter, and stored in memory. Our pixel time is yielded by dividing active line time by the number of pixels to be in the digital image line—39.44μS/256 = 154.1 nanoseconds (nS) or 39.44 μS/512 = 77.03nS. This time is critical in the design of the system, for it paces the speeds at which the A/D conversion must take place along with the rate at which data must be stored in memory.

To see the flow of the digitization process, we start at the vertical sync time. This sync signal indicates to the system that a field is beginning; assume it to be the even field. In either the 256-line or the 512-line case, the video counter is reset to zero. Digitization starts following the eleven no-video lines and the detection of the successive horizontal sync pulse. Horizontal sync indicates the start of a line. Once detected, the video pixel counter is reset to zero and the processor times out 6.575 μS, the inactive line time to form an image of 1:1 aspect ratio. Sampling begins, occurring repetitively at the interval prescribed by the number of pixels in the line. Once the correct number of pixels have been sampled, sampling stops and the next horizontal sync is awaited. During the sampling process, video information is converted to binary data and stored in memory. The arrival of the next vertical sync indicates the start of the odd field. For a 256-line system, this information is disregarded and the process becomes inactive until the following vertical sync. A 512-line system continues as before, sampling each line of the second field.

DIGITIZATION AND RECONSTRUCTION

The sampling operation of the previous section indicated to us the time at which video information was to be captured, digitized, and stored. In order to quantize the analog value of the video signal, we employ an A/D converter. Along with conversion of the incoming signal, it is also necessary to display an outgoing video signal. This is called *reconstruction* of the video image. The process is carried out with a digital to analog, or D/A, converter working in unison with the A/D conversion process. The difference is that the A/D data is being written into the image memory, whereas the D/A reads data out of the memory. As will be discussed later, suspension of the writing operation to memory leaves a frozen image for display and subsequent processing.

As we did with spatial resolution, we must define brightness quantization resolution to be handled by the system. Eight bits is most common; however, lower resolution may be acceptable or higher may be required by the application. As far as our hardware discussion goes, 4-, 6-, or 8-bit quantization resolutions may be handled as similar cases because of the availability of A/D and D/A converters in all three configurations.

The pixel times for 256 and 512 pixel lines were calculated to be 154.1nS and 77.03nS, respectively. These times determine the mandatory speeds at which the A/D and D/A converters must run. The A/D configuration is shown in Figure 6-5. The analog video signal is fed to the A/D and a *sync extractor*. The function of the sync extractor is to detect sync pulses within the video stream. Once detected, the extracted sync information is used by the system for timing and control purposes. Along with video, a strobe signal drives the A/D. The strobe, called PIXEL CLOCK, is pulsed at the time each sample is to be taken; in return, the A/D generates a binary value representing the analog input level. The strobe rate is at the frequency of $1/154.1nS = 6.5MHz$ for the 256-pixel-per-line case or $1/77.03nS = 13MHz$ for 512 pixels per line. These rates are fast by normal A/D standards and require the use of a type of A/D known as a flash converter.

Figure 6-5 Video A/D section block diagram.

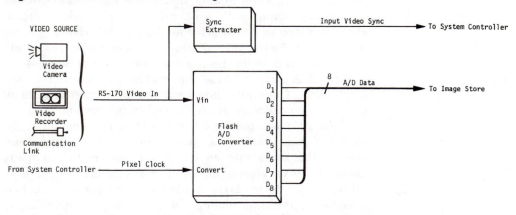

A flash A/D consists of individual voltage comparators for each input level to be detected and converted. For instance, a 6-bit converter requires 64 individual comparators. As resolution increases by 1 bit, the number of comparators double. Because of the density of these devices, they are considerably more expensive than the more conventional successive approximation devices.

Successive approximation A/Ds iterate using a single comparator to converge on the digital value representing the input level. They may take on the order of 1μS to complete the conversion. This is obviously too slow for our purposes, There is a tradeoff, however. In a system designed for low-cost applications where continuous digitization is not necessary, the successive approximation device may be used. This design uses the technique of digitizing one pixel per line time and takes a total of 256 frame times to acquire an entire 256 × 256 image. During one frame time, one pixel per line is converted during its active line time. Each successive frame, the pixel counter is incremented and the next set of pixels are converted. Of course, the tradeoff here is conversion time of an entire image. A 256 × 256 image will take 256 frame times, each

33.33 mS long, for a total time of 8.5 seconds. A 512×512 image will take twice as long. If the user can tolerate holding the original image stable in front of the camera this long, the design presents a viable alternative.

For our purposes, we will assume the use of a flash A/D allowing real-time digitization of an image in one frame time. This mode of implementation allows us to see the digitized image continuously on the display and offers much more versatility, as will become evident later. Flash A/D converters appropriate for use in our application have become quite common in recent years. One manufacturer, TRW, LSI Products Division, offers 4-, 6-, and 8-bit versions. Figure 6-6 illustrates these device specification sheets.

The reconstruction of a digital image, residing in memory, upon a display monitor is where we find the need for the D/A function. A D/A takes binary bits of data as input along with a strobe signal, PIXEL CLOCK, and generates the appropriate analog signal (see Figure 6-7). Mixing the analog output with sync information yields a reconstructed video signal to drive a standard television monitor for viewing. Again, the question of quantization resolution comes up. And again, from a hardware design point, 4- 6-, or 8-bit D/As are all available and may be used in a similar fashion. Generally, however, the D/A used will be of the same accuracy as the A/D used in the system.

As data are presented to the D/A from memory, the strobe signal, pixel clock, is generated. This signal operates at the same rate as the A/D's strobe and in many cases is the very same signal. The strobe latches the digital quantity into the D/A. In response, the converter generates the appropriate analog voltage level corresponding to the digital input. This level is sustained until the next strobe occurs. Figure 6-8 illustrates a typical high-speed 8-bit video D/A converter produced by TRW, LSI Products Division.

Our RS-170 video signal is now interfaced to the digital world. From this point on, all remaining data handling hardware is digital; the three major components are image memory, external computer interface, and internal image processor interface.

Image Storage

Probably the most space-consuming element of a digital image processor is the image memory, commonly referred to as the *image store*. It is here that the digitized image is stored for further use. Input and output data streams to the image store consist of video camera input, display monitor output, host computer input/output, and internal image processor hardware input/output. Further complicating the situation is the continual writing to and reading from memory required to capture and display video images. Timing constraints posed by video data rates require the image

TRW LSI PRODUCTS

Monolithic Video A/D Converter

4 Bit, 30 MSPS
Model: TDC1021J

The TRW TDC1021J is a 4 bit fully-parallel (flash) A/D converter capable of digitizing an analog signal at rates from dc to 30 megasamples per second (MSPS). It will accurately sample, without an external sample-and-hold circuit, input signals with full power bandwidths up to 10 MHz.

A single convert signal controls the unit operation, which consists of 15 sampling comparators, combining logic, and an output buffer register. Recovery from a full scale step input occurs within 20 nsec. Controls are provided for straight binary or offset two's complement output coding, in true or inverted sense.

The TDC1021J is patented (No. 3283170), with other patents pending. It is covered by TRW's standard 1-year limited warranty.

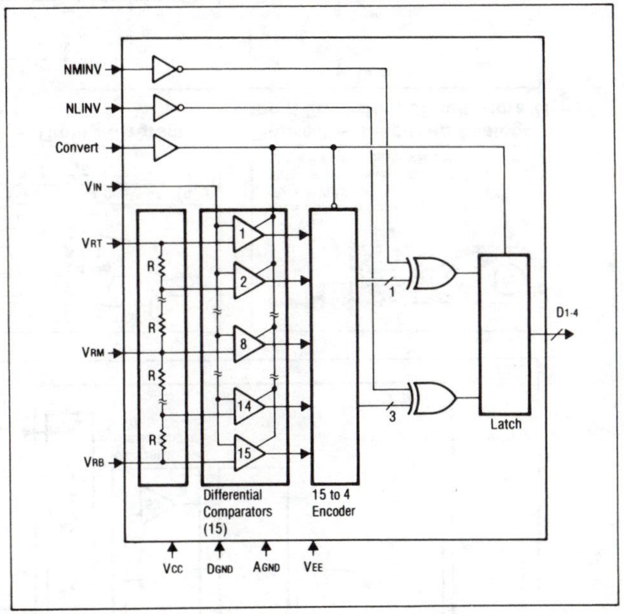

Features

- 4 bit resolution
- ±1/4 LSB linearity
- 30 MSPS
- No sample-and-hold circuit required
- Aperture jitter 30 psec
- Binary or two's complement output
- Monolithic, bipolar, TTL
- 16-pin ceramic DIP
- 250 mW power dissipation
- Commercial/military temperature range

Applications

- Video data conversion
- Radar data conversion
- High speed multiplexed data acquisition
- X-ray and ultrasound imaging
- Image processing
- Facsimile systems

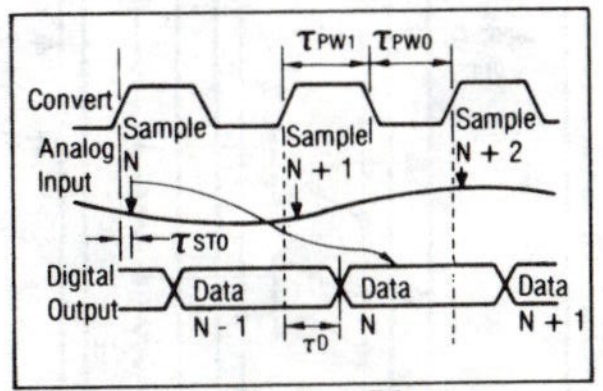

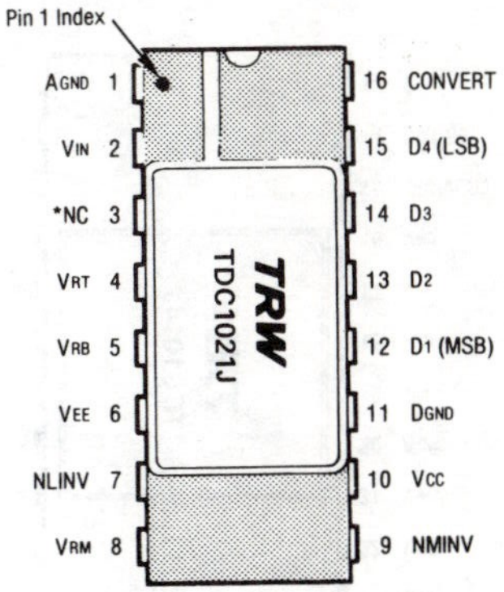

Figure 6-6
(a) Typical 4-bit flash A/D converter. (Reprinted by permission of TRW Inc., LSI Products Division, copyright © 1981.)

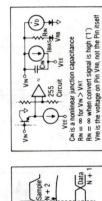

Figure 1 — Timing Diagram

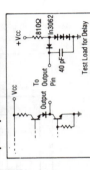

Figure 2 — Simplified Analog Input Equivalent Circuit

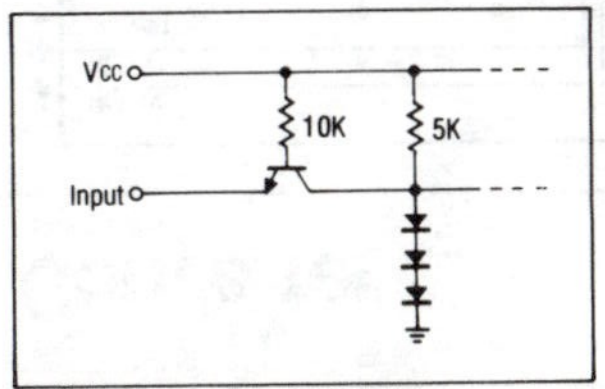

Figure 3 — Digital Input Equivalent Circuit

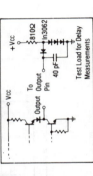

Figure 4 — Output Circuits

TRW LSI PRODUCTS

Monolithic Video A/D Converter

6 Bit, 30 MSPS
Model: TDC1014J

The TRW TDC1014J is a 6 bit fully-parallel (flash) A/D converter capable of digitizing an analog signal at rates from dc to 30 megasamples per second (MSPS). It will accurately sample, without an external sample-and-hold circuit, input signals with full power bandwidths up to 10 MHz.

A single convert signal controls the unit operation, which consists of 63 sampling comparators, combining logic, and an output buffer register. Recovery from a full scale step input occurs within 20 nsec. Controls are provided for straight binary or offset two's complement output coding, in true or inverted sense.

The TDC1014J is patented (No. 3283170), with other patents pending. It is covered by TRW's standard 1-year limited warranty.

Features

- 6 bit resolution
- ±1/4 LSB linearity
- 30 MSPS
- No sample-and-hold circuit required
- Aperture jitter 30 psec
- Binary or two's complement output
- Monolithic, bipolar, TTL
- 24-pin ceramic DIP
- 0.75W power dissipation

Applications

- Video data conversion
- Radar data conversion
- High speed multiplexed data acquisition
- X-ray and ultrasound imaging
- Image processing

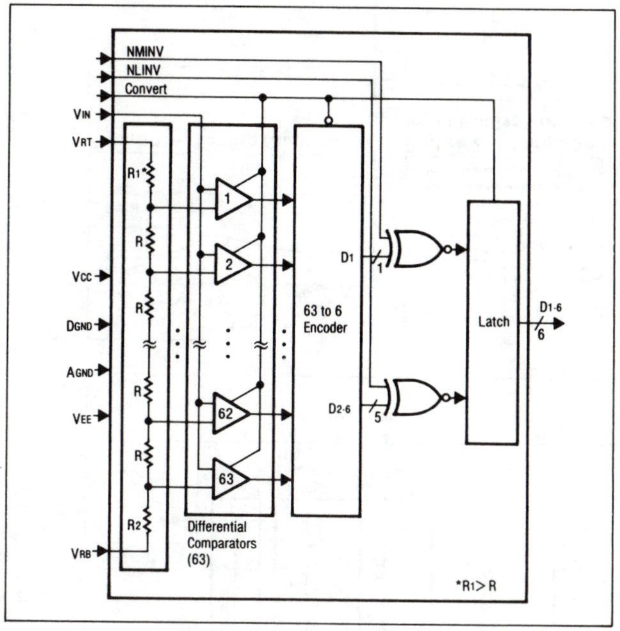

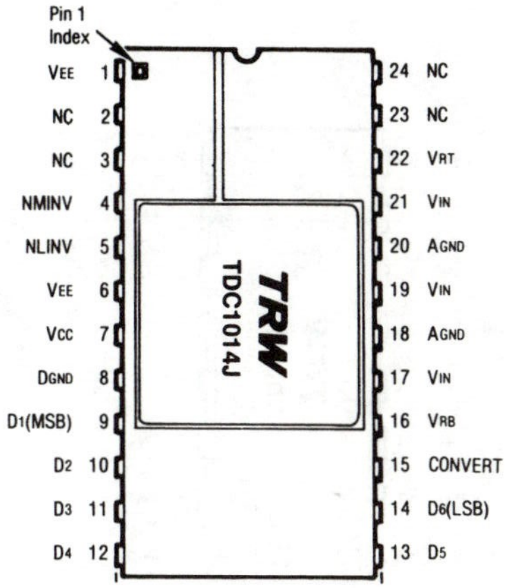

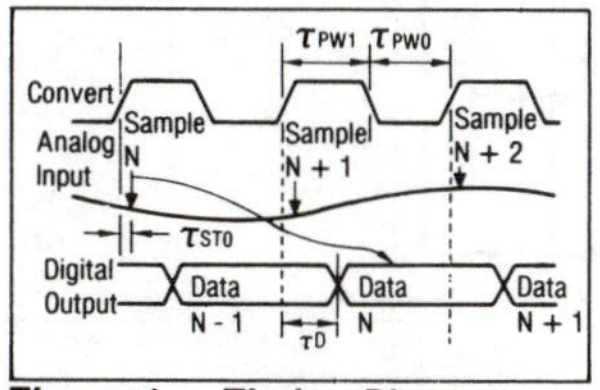

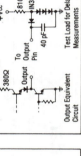

Figure 1 — Timing Diagram (Note 1)

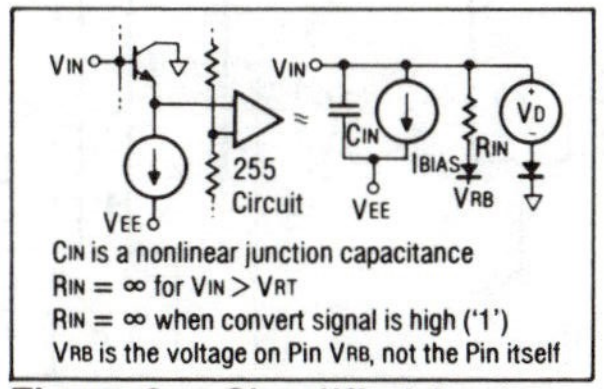

Figure 2 — Simplified Analog Input Equivalent Circuit (Note 2)

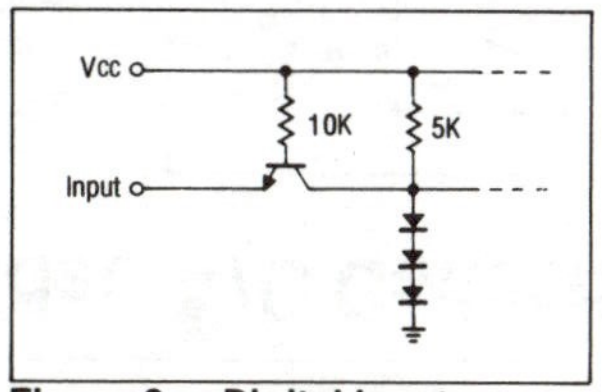

Figure 3 — Digital Input Equivalent Circuit

Figure 4 — Output Circuits

(b) Typical 6-bit flash A/D converter. (Reprinted by permission of TRW Inc., LSI Products Division, copyright © 1981.)

TRW *LSI PRODUCTS*

Monolithic Video A/D Converter

8 BIT, 30 MSPS
Model: TDC1007J

The TRW TDC1007J is an 8 bit fully-parallel (flash) A/D converter capable of digitizing an analog signal at rates from dc to 30 mega-samples per second (MSPS). It will accurately sample, without an external sample-and-hold circuit, input signals with full power bandwidths up to 10 MHz.

A single convert signal controls the unit operation, which consists of 255 sampling comparators, combining comparators, com-bining logic, and an output buffer register. Recovery from a full scale step input occurs within 20 nsec. Controls are provided for straight binary or offset two's complement output coding, in true or inverted sense.

The TDC1007J is patented (No. 3283170), with other patents pending. It is covered by TRW's standard 1-year limited warranty.

Features

- 8 bit resolution
- 30 MSPS
- No sample-and-hold circuit required
- Aperture jitter 30 psec
- Differential phase 0.5°
- Differential gain 1.5%
- Binary or two's complement
- Monolithic, bipolar, TTL
- 64-pin ceramic DIP
- 2.0W power dissipation

Applications

- Video data conversion
- 3X or 4X NTSC color
- 3X or 4X PAL color
- Radar data conversion
- High speed multiplexed data acquisition

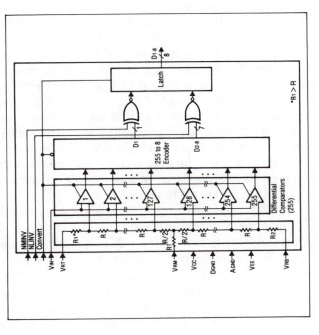

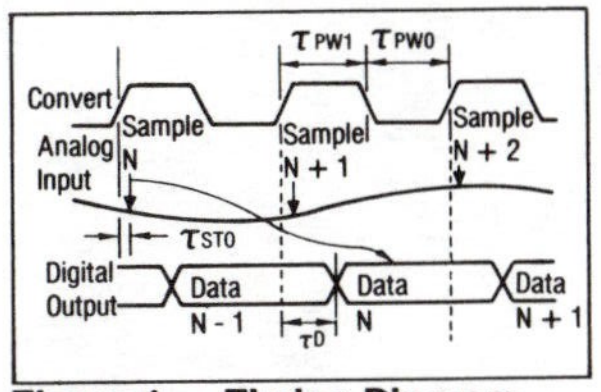

*R₁ > R

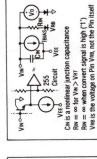

Figure 1 — Timing Diagram (Note 1)

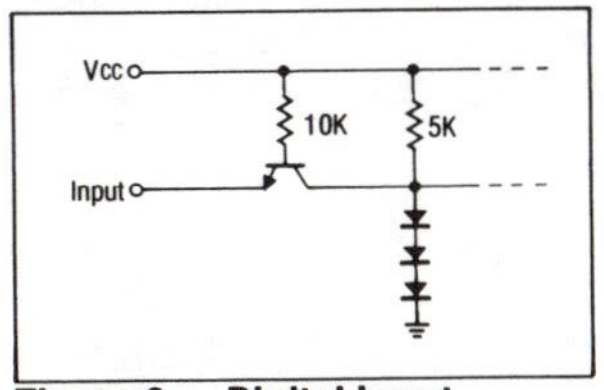

Figure 3 — Digital Input Equivalent Circuit

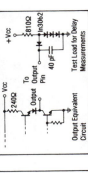

Cin is a nonlinear junction capacitance
Rin = ∞ for Vin > Vrt
Rin = ∞ when convert signal is high ('1')
Vrb is the voltage on Pin Vrb, not the Pin itself

Figure 2 — Simplified Analog Input Equivalent Circuit (Note 2)

Output Equivalent Circuit

Test Load for Delay Measurements

Figure 4 — Output Circuits

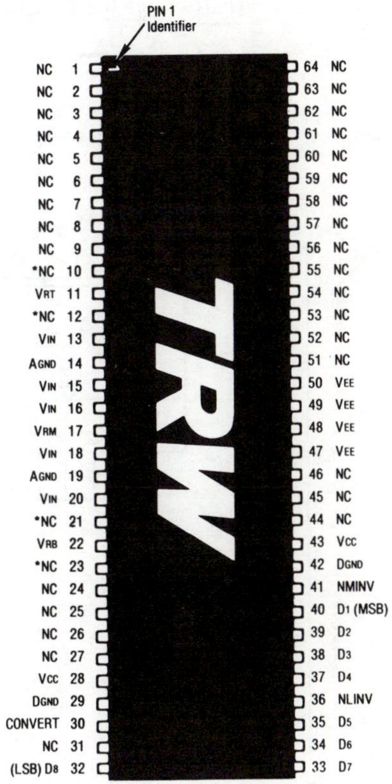

(c) Typical 8-bit flash A/D converter. (Reprinted by permission of TRW Inc., LSI Products Division, copyright © 1981.)

81

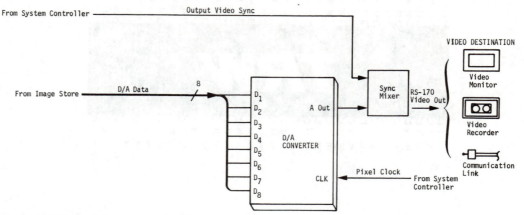

Figure 6-7 Video D/A section block diagram.

store architecture to reflect special techniques of data buffering and control. In this section, we will discuss specific techniques along with general implementations of video image store design.

To begin this discussion, let us first consider image memory size. An image with a spatial resolution of 256 lines by 256 pixels is quantized to eight bits per pixel. The storage of this image will require a memory array capable of storing $256 \times 256 \times 8$ bits or a total of 524,288 bits of information. An image of $512 \times 512 \times 8$ bits requires four times the memory, or 2,097,152 bits. To make these storage figures a little more manageable, we often indicate memory needs in pixel-wise quantities where, in this case, the pixel is equal to eight bits. Therefore, our 256×256 image requires 65,536 pixels of storage space in memory; 262,144 pixels for a 512×512 image.

When considering an 8-bit pixel, we may also use the term *byte* to describe the storage space of a pixel's brightness. A byte is defined as a data quantity of eight bits and is a term commonly encountered when discussing computer systems. Looking at the case of the 256×256 image, we see that 65,536 bytes are necessary for storage. To place this storage figure in perspective, it represents the entire memory capacity of many standard personal computers. Also, when digitizing 256 pixels in a line, there is the equivalent of a new pixel to be stored in memory every 154.1nS—hardly within the capability of a home computer. We see from this brief analysis that the storage of an image requires a great deal of fast memory.

The memory to be used is known as *random access memory,* or RAM. Of available RAMs, there are two varieties, *static* and *dynamic.* Static RAMs have attributes of random data storage and retrieval with a minimum of support circuitry. Once the data is written, it stays as long as power is applied. Dynamic RAMs, on the other hand, must be continually refreshed so that they don't forget what is stored within them. Refreshing is accomplished by the sequential reading of certain locations within each chip ev-

TRW *LSI PRODUCTS*

Monolithic Video D/A Converters

8, 9, 10 Bit, 20 MSPS

Models:
TDC1016J-8
TDC1016JM-8
TDC1016J-9
TDC1016J-10

The TRW TDC1016J-8/9/10 bit D/A converters are capable of converting a digital signal into an analog voltage at the rate of 20 megasamples per second (MSPS). No external input register, deglitching, or resampling is needed. No operational amplifier or buffer is required at the analog output.

All parts have 10 bits of active digital input. Three accuracy grades are offered: 8, 9, 10 bits. Simply grounding the Vcc terminal causes the inputs to become ECL compatible.

The TDC1016J is patented (U.S. Patent No. 3283170) with other patents pending.

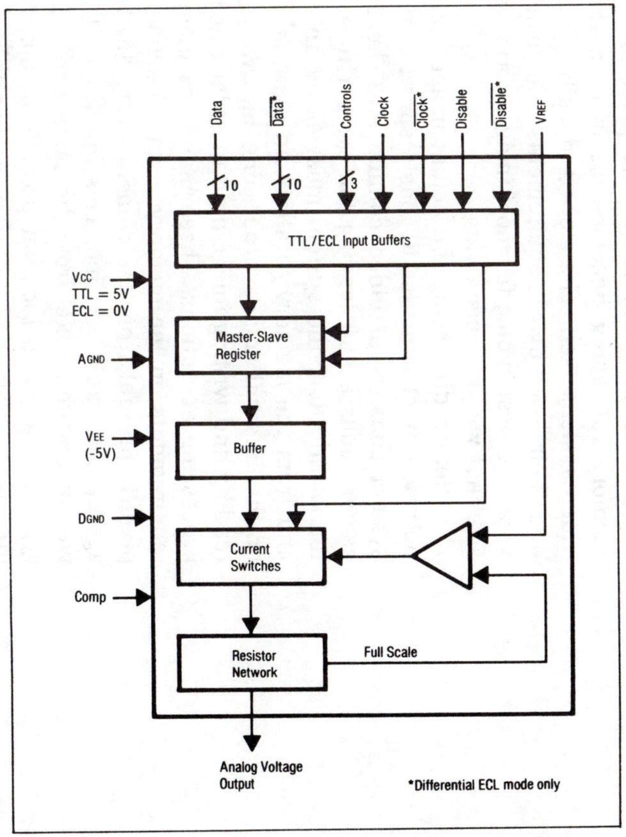

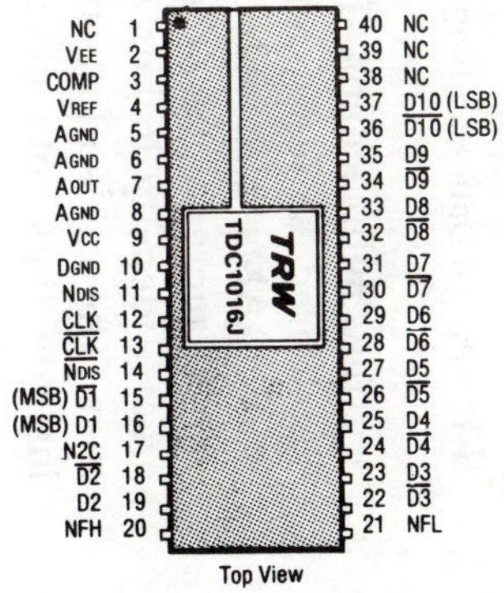

Features

- 8, 9, and 10 bit accuracy
- 20 MSPS
- Voltage output
- ECL or TTL inputs (only −5.0V supply required for ECL mode)
- Single ended or differential ECL inputs
- All data registered on chip
- No deglitching circuit required
- Output disable capability
- Differential phase: 0.5°
- Differential gain: 1.0%
- Binary or two's complement input
- Zero and full scale control for easy calibration
- Data inversion control
- Monolithic, bipolar
- 40 pin ceramic DIP
- 0.6W power dissipation
- MIL STD 883 screening available

Applications

- Video data conversion
  3X or 4X NTSC color
  3X or 4X PAL color
- Color/B & W graphics
- CRT displays
- Waveform/test signal generation

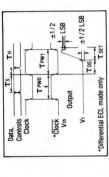

Figure 6-8 Typical 8-bit high-speed D/A converter. (Reprinted by permission of TRW Inc., LSI Products Division, copyright © 1981.)

Figure 1 — Timing Diagram

83

ery few milliseconds. This refreshing requirement is often considered a design difficulty in most memory systems. Static RAMs, although they are easy to use, require considerably more power than dynamics and do not offer as great a density in bits per chip, due to larger chip geometries. The tradeoffs between static and dynamic RAMs illustrate that both offer good and bad points, depending upon the application.

It just so happens that dynamic RAMs are ideally suited for the application of video image storage. Not only are power requirements and overall array size kept to a minimum, but refreshing is not a problem because of a need to continually read memory anyway, in order to update the display monitor. Because the system must keep an image on the display monitor at all times, sequential reading of all memory locations takes place every 33.33mS, and memory refreshing becomes an inherent function of the video system itself. The storage density of dynamic RAMs and their low power requirements add to make these devices the best choice for most image storage systems of the size that we are considering.

Before discussing the actual image memory architecture, we must consider its basic speed requirements. Our system consists of video coming into the system from a camera source and leaving the system to a display monitor. In addition, the system must allow an access path to and from the memory to allow an external host computer or the internal image processing hardware a method of reading and writing image data in order to carry out image processing operations. These mandates place tough speed requirements on the memory array. We saw earlier that a pixel is present from the camera every 154.1nS for an image of 256 pixels per line. This implies that every 154.1nS we must write a pixel from the camera to the image memory, read the same location pixel from the memory to the display monitor, and, as often as possible, allow external read or write accesses to the memory for either the host computer or the internal image processor. Of course, the time allowed to carry out these operations for 512 pixels per line is halved. All these operations in 154.1nS, or 77.03nS for the 512-pixel-per-line case, is difficult to imagine, but as we will see, there are definite memory design techniques available in which to handle the requirement.

THE TWO-PORT MEMORY CONCEPT

The design of an image store requires utilization of two techniques in the memory architecture. One technique is that of a two-port memory design. As we saw earlier, video data from the image memory must be accepted from a camera and presented to a display monitor continuously to provide an uninterrupted picture. This requirement would permanently tie up the memory data access path in a conventional memory design. Since we wish to allow additional external accessing to the image data so that internal or external image processing may occur, we must provide a second memory access path. This allows the memory to be accessed without interrupting the camera and display image data flow. This second access path to the memory is handled by implementing a two-port memory design.

The other technique used is that of video data buffering, so that larger amounts of video information may be accessed in and out of memory at the same time. By buffering the brightness data of several pixels prior to or following the accessing of the image memory, the number of data bits transferred to the memory in a certain amount of time may be increased. This in turn allows both data paths to the two-port memory to operate in an interleaved manner without conflicting. This buffering technique is discussed in the following section.

Let us review the need for a two-port memory design. Video information is continuously going into and out of the image memory, or image store. The system user wishes to freeze the current camera image in memory and carry out various image processes on the frozen image. When the image is frozen, camera input is no longer of concern; however, the display monitor must still be updated with the image in memory. This requires continual accessing of the image store to read data to be given to the D/A for ultimate display. If image processing is to happen, the system processing hardware also wishes to access the memory to read data, process it, and return the results. If we allow the processing hardware to take precedence over the display circuitry and access memory whenever it chooses, image data to be displayed will occasionally be pre-empted from coming out of memory and, in the end, never be displayed. This causes the display monitor to show holes, in a random pattern of lost data. This appears as visual static, or "snow," on the monitor and is not preferred.

On the other hand, video data are not being generated during sync and blanked times. Recalling earlier, every line in a 1:1 image has $6.575\mu S$ of blanked time on either side of the active line and $10.9\mu S$ of sync time per line. Therefore, there is a total of $24.05\mu S$ of inactive video time per line. For this length of time during each line of video, image memory is not required for use by the display circuitry. We may use this time to allow access to image memory by either the host computer or internal image processing hardware. The question is, does this amount of access time allow expedient processing of an image? The answer is generally no.

Various processing algorithms, as discussed in Part II, require different amounts of time to carry out the operation. On a pixel-by-pixel basis, these times vary widely; therefore, required accesses to the image memory also vary. If the processor completes a particular calculation—

say, at the start of an active line time—it must wait the duration of the active time, 39.44μS. These waits will result in the image processing hardware becoming *input/output bound*—meaning that it spends more time trying to get and replace data to the image store than processing the data itself.

To yield considerably more power out of an image processing system with only a slight increase in system cost, it is more advantageous to implement a two-port memory design. This architecture provides two independent data access paths to the image store. The concept breaks image store memory cycles into two subcycles. The first subcycle, called the video input/output subcycle, allows video camera data to be written into the image store while video display data are read out. The second subcycle, called the external input/output subcycle, provides read/write access to the image store by either the host computer or internal image processing hardware. With this scheme, the processing hardware is allowed to access the image store as often as the display circuitry. The idea here is that the display electronics must grab several pixels out of the image store each time it is allowed access so that it may then sequence them out over the period of time that the second subcycle is tying up the memory. Figure 6-9 illustrates the timing of the two-port memory scheme. Later in this chapter we will discuss actual times involved in the two-port scheme, making clear how this method reduces input/output overhead for the processing hardware.

IMAGE DATA TO MEMORY BUFFERING

To implement shared access to an image memory, time becomes the critical element. We have pixels coming into and out of the system at a rate of one every 154.1nS (we will dwell on the 256 × 256 image case). Additionally, we must allow the second access to the memory on a periodic basis.

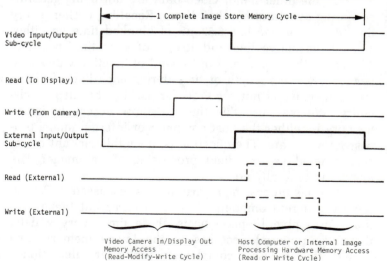

Figure 6-9 Basic timing diagram for the two-port image store memory access scheme.

The limiting factor is memory cycle time, or how fast a particular memory chip will access two random data locations. In order not to exceed this limit, we buffer the image data going in and out of memory, accessing several pixels' worth of data in memory every allowed access cycle.

Dynamic RAM memory chips come with a variety of timing specifications that must be met by the driving electronics if the devices are to work properly. An important specification to us is *cycle time,* the total amount of time needed to access random data and prepare the chip for a following access. Along with the wide variety of available chips come an equally wide variety of cycle time specifications. To make things easier, we will assume for the moment that we are using chips with a 300nS cycle time. The next section will tie together these topics concerning the image store and will deal more specifically with actual cycle times.

The memory is organized around two subcycles, as described in the previous section. The first subcycle uses a dynamic RAM Read-Modify-Write cycle, whereas the second subcycle is either a standard Read or Write cycle. The Read-Modify-Write cycle allows the system to read a location of memory followed by an immediate write to the same location. For us, this means that pixels are read and passed on to the display monitor driving circuitry followed by a write of data collected from the camera input. This cycle takes about as long as a single Read or Write cycle, yet allows both the camera input and display output operations to occur. Our second subcycle is reserved for a Read or Write to image memory by either the host computer or the internal image processing hardware. So, assuming both subcycles to be 300nS in length, we have an overall memory cycle of 600nS.

The problem is how to carry out 600nS cycles through memory in the allotted 154.1nS as defined by the pixel time. Actually, pixel data are not handled one by one; instead, we use the technique called pixel buffering. By collecting four pixels from the A/D and writing them all simultaneously into memory, the time between writes will be $4 \times 154.1nS = 616.4nS$. Using the Read-Modify-Write cycle, four pixels are also read out of the memory in the same cycle. These pixels are latched and then sequenced out to the D/A every 154.1nS. The Read-Modify-Write memory cycle takes 300nS, leaving another 300nS + to do either a Read or Write, as necessary, before the next Read-Modify-Write must occur. This scheme not only allows continual picture capture and display but also gives external access to the image memory once every 600nS.

In actual implementation of the buffering scheme, there are four pixel latches, between the A/D and the image store and between the image store and the D/A. Looking at the output buffer section, the idea is that four pixels are sequenced out of the four-pixel buffer to the

D/A. Just after the last of the four pixels is strobed into the D/A, the buffer is loaded from memory with the next four pixels to go out. This loading and sequencing continues in a cyclic manner, never interrupting the flow of pixel data to the D/A even though the image store is only accessed once every four pixel times. The analogous operation takes place in the input section.

Another method that utilizes the same timing strategy as the buffering scheme without the need for buffers is known as *phased memory access.* The cycles as previously outlined are all the same, but rather than writing to memory in blocks of four pixels, each 8-bit pixel section of the 32-bit wide memory width is skewed by one quarter of the total memory cycle time of 600nS. This allows pixels to sequentially load into each of the four banks of memory yet preserves the overall cycle time of 600nS each. Each of the four 8-bit banks operates through the original cycle scheme, but out of phase by one quarter cycle time of the adjacent banks. This scheme requires four separate memory timing circuits, one for each bank. This tradeoff often makes the pixel buffer technique more attractive. Figure 6-10 outlines the timing of the phased memory access method.

Figure 6-10 Basic timing diagram for the phased memory access scheme.

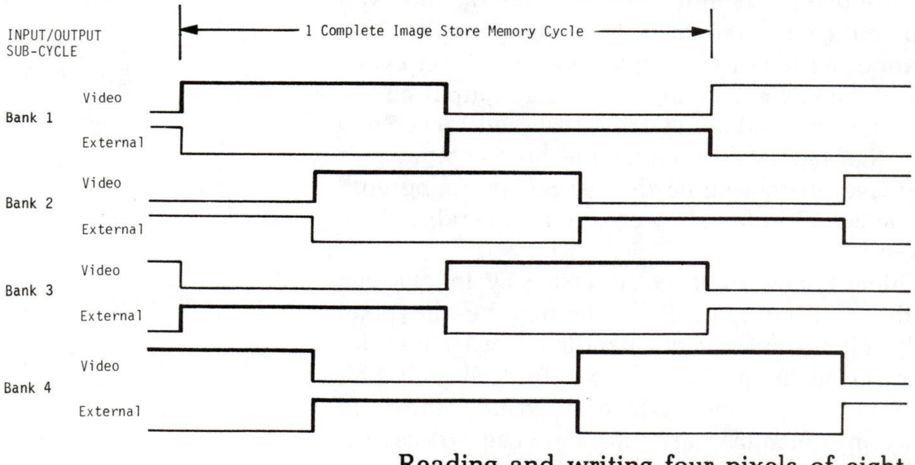

Reading and writing four pixels of eight bits each to memory simultaneously indicates that 32 bits are transferred to memory at once. This data transfer size is referred to as memory *data bandwidth* and has important implications for memory architecture and the chips to be used. For instance, if we were to choose 64K $\times$ 1 bit RAM chips, a 256 $\times$ 256 image of 8-bit pixels would fit neatly into eight chips. The only problem—a major one, at that—is that only eight bits may be written or read at a time. Since a new 8-bit quantity, or pixel, is available every 154.1nS we have a problem with cycling through memory fast enough—remember, two 300nS cycles are needed. Therefore, we must choose chips of the same overall size but different architecture. A 16K $\times$ 4-bit chip would fit the application well. Eight of these devices give 32 bits in and out of the chip, allowing four pixels to be buffered and loaded in and out of the image memory simultaneously. Image store architecture will be discussed further in the next section.

The integration of pixel buffering and two-port memory access yields an image store design capable of continuous video input and output along with external device memory access. The most appealing aspect of this type of architecture is the external access of an image data once every 600nS. To pull these concepts together and lay out a total image store design, we continue to the next section.

BASIC IMAGE STORE DESIGN

We will now consider the image store as a component block element of the image processing system. Mating this block with the A/D and D/A blocks seen earlier, it is possible for our system to capture, display, and store images. Adding internal image processing hardware to an external host computer and their associated interfaces yields an entire system capable of carrying out image processing tasks. Image archiving and more elaborate processing are available through the use of the host computer system.

The image store utilizes two design concepts—a two-port access scheme and input/output data buffering. As discussed previously, these techniques allow quick processor access to the store as well as the data bandwidth necessary to capture and display the relatively fast video data that we are dealing with. In order to carry out the design of an image store, however, we must fully understand the operational modes of dynamic RAMs. From this point, then, we may discuss various designs for 256×256 and 512×512 image stores.

Dynamic RAMs are available in a variety of sizes and configurations. The most popular RAM sizes for our purpose are $16K \times 1$-bit and $16K \times 4$-bit devices. Of course, higher density devices are becoming available at an increasing pace, making older designs somewhat obsolete. For now we will be concerned only with the two sizes listed. Since both size and data width of a particular RAM play an important part in our design, we find that as the overall size of the RAM is increased, so must the data width. As in the example cited earlier, a $256 \times 256 \times 8$-bit image fits into eight $64K \times 1$-bit RAMs just fine, but the data bandwidth is limited to eight bits, or one pixel, per RAM cycle. This, combined with basic cycle times of dynamic RAMs, will not allow us to get our image data in and out of the RAM at video rates, making the $64K \times 8$-bit RAM architecture not suitable for our application.

Dynamic RAMs operate in a variety of modes, or cycles, the most common of which are Read, Write and Read-Modify-Write. Additionally, cycles called Page Mode

Read, Page Mode Write, and Page Mode Read-Modify-Write are available and useful to us in some designs. A final cycle called Refresh allows the refreshing of storage elements within the circuit, a mandatory requirement of dynamic RAMs.

In dealing with dynamic RAMs the necessity to refresh the memory within a certain period of time is everpresent. However, in lieu of using the Refresh cycle, refreshing may also be effected by continual Read cycles, or Read-Modify-Write cycles, accessing the appropriate locations within the memory chip. We will find that in our case, refreshing is accomplished automatically due to the continual and repetitive cycling through memory to keep the image on the display monitor. For this reason, we need not rely on the actual Refresh cycle.

Electrically, dynamic RAM chips consist of signal lines for Address, Data In, Data Out, Row Address Strobe, Column Address Strobe, and Write Enable. The specification sheet for the Intel 2118, a 16K $\times$ 1 dynamic RAM, is shown in Figure 6-11. For this RAM, seven address lines go into the chip. To address a particular bit of the 16,384 available within the RAM, 14 address bits are necessary. The scheme employed in getting all 14 address bits into the RAM is to place seven on the address lines (A0-A6) and pulse the Row Address Strobe ($\overline{\text{RAS}}$) line. The other seven address bits are then put on the address lines, followed by a pulse on the Column Address Strobe ($\overline{\text{CAS}}$) line. The RAM latches all 14 address bits internally in two steps as the $\overline{\text{RAS}}$ and $\overline{\text{CAS}}$ lines are strobed. Depending upon the condition of the Write Enable ($\overline{\text{WE}}$) line, the RAM then either writes data from the Data In (DIN) line to the addressed internal memory location or reads data out to the Data Out (DOUT) line.

A Read cycle is handled by strobing in seven bits of row address information followed by seven bits of column address. Remember, these row and column addresses do not relate to the line and pixel addresses of our stored image. With the $\overline{\text{WE}}$ line held inactive, the RAM outputs one bit of data on the DOUT line. A Write cycle is similar, but now the $\overline{\text{WE}}$ line is driven active at the appropriate time. The RAM accepts one bit of data from the DIN line and writes it to the appropriate internal location. A Read-Modify-Write cycle incorporates both the Read and Write cycles into one, using the same address information for both operations. This buys time in that the address is strobed in only once for both a Read and Write. As in the Read cycle, address information is strobed in. The RAM replies by outputting one bit of data from the addressed internal location to the DOUT line. At this point, the $\overline{\text{WE}}$ line must be taken to the active level forcing the RAM to write into the location just read with one bit of data presented on the DIN line. Since the bulk of time involved in all dynamic RAM cycles is dedicated to address strobing, we have been allowed to do a Read and Write in about half the time it

intel

2118 FAMILY
16,384 x 1 BIT DYNAMIC RAM

	2118-10	2118-12	2118-15
Maximum Access Time (ns)	100	120	150
Read, Write Cycle (ns)	235	270	320
Read-Modify-Write Cycle (ns)	285	320	410

- **Single +5V Supply, ±10% Tolerance**
- **HMOS Technology**
- **Low Power: 150 mW Max. Operating**
  11 mW Max. Standby
- **Low V_{DD} Current Transients**
- **All Inputs, Including Clocks, TTL Compatible**

- **$\overline{CAS}$ Controlled Output is Three-State, TTL Compatible**
- **$\overline{RAS}$ Only Refresh**
- **128 Refresh Cycles Required Every 2ms**
- **Page Mode and Hidden Refresh Capability**
- **Allows Negative Overshoot V_{IL} min = -2V**

The Intel® 2118 is a 16,384 word by 1-bit Dynamic MOS RAM designed to operate from a single +5V power supply. The 2118 is fabricated using HMOS — a production proven process for high performance, high reliability, and high storage density.

The 2118 uses a single transistor dynamic storage cell and advanced dynamic circuitry to achieve high speed with low power dissipation. The circuit design minimizes the current transients typical of dynamic RAM operation. These low current transients contribute to the high noise immunity of the 2118 in a system environment.

Multiplexing the 14 address bits into the 7 address input pins allows the 2118 to be packaged in the industry standard 16-pin DIP. The two 7-bit address words are latched into the 2118 by the two TTL clocks, Row Address Strobe ($\overline{RAS}$) and Column Address Strobe ($\overline{CAS}$). Non-critical timing requirements for $\overline{RAS}$ and $\overline{CAS}$ allow use of the address multiplexing technique while maintaining high performance.

The 2118 three-state output is controlled by $\overline{CAS}$, independent of $\overline{RAS}$. After a valid read or read-modify-write cycle, data is latched on the output by holding $\overline{CAS}$ low. The data out pin is returned to the high impedance state by returning $\overline{CAS}$ to a high state. The 2118 hidden refresh feature allows $\overline{CAS}$ to be held low to maintain latched data while $\overline{RAS}$ is used to execute $\overline{RAS}$-only refresh cycles.

The single transistor storage cell requires refreshing for data retention. Refreshing is accomplished by performing $\overline{RAS}$-only refresh cycles, hidden refresh cycles, or normal read or write cycles on the 128 address combinations of A_0 through A_6 during a 2ms period. A write cycle will refresh stored data on all bits of the selected row except the bit which is addressed.

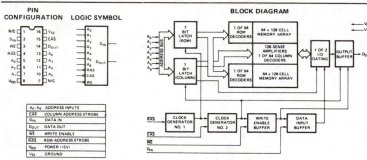

Figure 6-11 Typical 16K × 1-bit dynamic RAM. (Reprinted by permission of Intel Corporation, copyright © 1980.)

would have taken if we had done a normal Read cycle followed by a Write cycle. For the purposes of an image store, the Read-Modify-Write cycle allows image memory to be read (sending data to the D/A) and written (with data coming from the A/D) in an expedient manner. Figure 6-12 illustrates the basic timing for the three cycles.

The other three cycles of interest in some image store designs are the Page Mode versions of the above-cited cycles. In the 16K × 1 dynamic RAM, 7 of the 14 address bits are the row address and the remaining 7 bits, the column address. A page is defined as all the memory locations having a common row address. In other words, there are $2^7 = 128$ pages of $2^7 = 128$ locations, or bits, in the 16K × 1-bit RAM. In applying the Page mode to reading locations within the boundaries of a common page, the three cycles—Read, Write, and Read-Modify-Write, require that row address information be strobed in only once. Subsequent cycles must only strobe in the column address; the row address stays latched internally in the RAM. As a re-

91

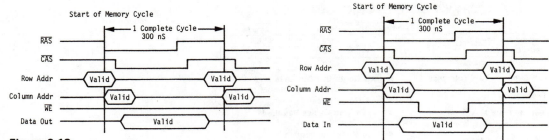

Figure 6-12
(a) Basic Dynamic RAM Read cycle timing diagram. (b) Write cycle timing diagram.

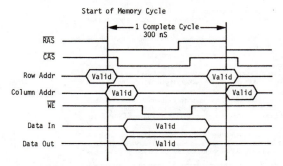

(c) Read-Modify-Write cycle timing diagram.

Figure 6-13
(a) Basic Dynamic RAM Page mode Read
cycle timing diagram.

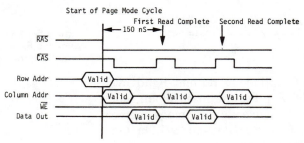

(b) Page mode Write cycle timing diagram.

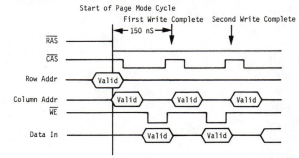

(c) Page mode Read-Modify cycle timing diagram.

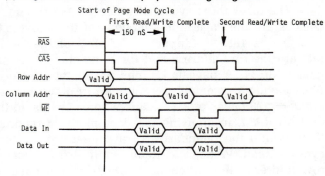

sult, cycle times may be cut roughly in half over those of normal cycles. The three Page Mode cycles are shown in Figure 6-13.

The necessity of dynamic RAM refreshing requires the user of these devices to understand the internal mechanics involved. Within a dynamic RAM exists an array of locations capable of storing a single bit of digital information. Each location may take on the value of either a "1" or a "0." This digital value is stored as a charge on a capacitor-like element with the aid of a single transistor. For instance, a "1" may be stored as the presence of some charge appearing between the capacitor and ground whereas a "0" would be the absence of a charge. The phenomenon encountered is that the charge tends to leak off due to the extremely small geometric size of the capacitor. So after a while, the charge left by writing a "1" to a particular location will diminish to the point that it is read back as a "0." In order to insure that a charge will not slip below the threshold of a "1" to a "0," it is necessary to perform refreshing.

Refreshing is carried out on an internal row-by-row basis. Whenever a row address is strobed into the RAM by way of the $\overline{RAS}$ line, followed by the normal execution of a valid cycle, the entire internal row of 128 locations becomes refreshed. Referring back to the block diagram of the 2118, we note that internally the RAM is set up as two 64×128 cell arrays. Any given row address enables 64 cells from each array to pass to the 128 sense amplifiers. The column address allows one to pass through to the output amplifier and on to the DOUT signal line. In addition, the 128 bits present at the sense amps are amplified and returned to the original capacitor storage elements. It is this feedback path that restores the charge on each capacitor to the full charge level of either a "1" or a "0."

Since the charge tends to leak off the memory storage elements, there is a definite period of time that must not be exceeded before any given cell is refreshed. For the average dynamic RAM, this time is on the order of 2mS. This means that within 2mS each and every one of the 128 rows must be accessed in one way or another. As we will see shortly, it turns out that this requirement may be handled very simply in our application. With a little forethought in the designing of an image memory, refreshing becomes an inherent feature, due to necessity of continual reading of image data to be displayed on the monitor.

We are ready to consider the design of a 256×256 image store. At this point we will assume dynamic RAM Read, Write, and Read-Modify-Write cycles all take 300nS. This is a fair assumption, in that some devices are slower and some faster. Also, every year these parts become available in faster versions. The first step is to define overall memory capacity. Dealing with 8-bit pixels, this figure will be $256 \times 256 \times 8 = 524,288$ bits. Next we figure overall memory cycle time to allow a two-port operation. This will be a Read-Modify-Write subcycle followed by a Read or Write subcycle. The two subcycles make up the overall image store cycle, $2 \times 300nS = 600nS$. With the constraint of 256 pixels per line, how many 154.1nS pixels must be buffered before cycling in and out of memory? 600nS memory cycle time/154.1nS pixel time = 3.9 pixels/memory cycle; this is rounded up to four pixels per memory cycle. The overall memory cycle then becomes 4 pixels $\times$ 154.1nS = 616.4nS. Our image store bandwidth must therefore be 4 pixels $\times$ 8-bits/pixel = 32 bits, meaning that we will always cycle 32-bit chunks in and out of memory during any given cycle. If we decide now to use 16K $\times$ 1-bit chips, it is clear that 32 chips would be needed to get the required bandwidth. Furthermore, by taking the overall required storage capacity of 524,288 bits divided by the 32-bit bandwidth, each chip must have the capacity of 524,288/32 = 16,384 bits. It works out perfectly: 32 16K $\times$ 1-bit chips not only gives us a bandwidth of 32 bits, but also allows an overall capacity of 524,288 bits. The memory requirements are now defined.

One item must be confirmed, however, before we commit to the design—the time for a total refresh of all memory to occur. Every four pixel times, two memory subcycles are performed. The Read-Modify-Write cycle is sequential, meaning that the address increments by one each cycle. This is because image data to the display monitor or from a camera is, by definition, pixel-by-pixel, line-by-line. The other subcycle is random, determined by what the host computer or internal image processing hardware wishes to use. Therefore, we may say that every four pixel times we will accomplish one of the 128 refreshes during the Read-Modify-Write subcycle. The second subcycle does indeed do a refresh but since it randomly accesses memory we are never guaranteed that all refreshing will be done. Given 256 pixels in a line of video data we see that 256 pixels/4 pixels per memory cycle = 64 refreshes occur every video line time. So, every two video line times all 128 refreshes occur. As noted earlier, a video line time is $63.49\mu S$ in duration; therefore, 128 refreshes occur in $127.0\mu S$—well within the 2mS limit. The only constraint imposed by the refreshing requirement is that the seven row addresses strobed in by the $\overline{RAS}$ signal must be the least significant address bits of the video address counters. These are the bits that increment every video access memory cycle time, insuring that all 128 RAM locations are refreshed every 128 accesses.

Figure 6-14 illustrates the 256 $\times$ 256, 16K $\times$ 1-bit RAM image store block diagram. The three elements are a four-pixel input buffer, a four-pixel output buffer, and thirty-two 16K $\times$ 1-bit dynamic RAMs.

The 256 $\times$ 256 $\times$ 8 bit image store considered here is in its basic form. There are a few enhancements that can reduce chip count and yield a somewhat cleaner and more elegant design. The first, and most obvious, enhancement

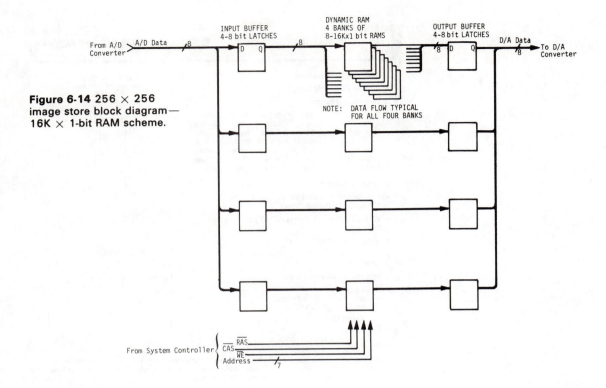

Figure 6-14 256 × 256 image store block diagram — 16K × 1-bit RAM scheme.

is found in the consideration of using 64K RAMs instead of the 16K RAMs chosen. To go to a 64K version, we first note that there is an increased chip storage density of four to one. Therefore, instead of thirty-two 16K RAM chips, there will be only eight 64K chips. This poses the problem of data bandwidth in and out of the memory, which has already been defined as having to be 32 bits. Using eight 64K × 1-bit chips, we only get a bandwidth of eight bits—not enough. The alternative is to use 16K × 4-bit versions of the 64K RAM type. The specification sheet for the Texas Instruments TMS 4416, a 16K × 4-bit dynamic RAM, is shown in Figure 6-15. Eight of these chips give us the 32-bit bandwidth necessary. In fact, we may visualize the single 16K × 4-bit RAM as directly replacing four of the original 16K × 1-bit RAMs. The upgrade to 64K RAMs of the 16K × 4-bit variety nets us a reduction in physical memory size of four to one. This represents an excellent savings in printed circuit board space, affording a more tidy package carrying out the identical function as before. Figure 6-16 illustrates the 64K RAM version of our image store.

A second, more subtle upgrade, known as phased memory access, was discussed earlier. This method reduces the number of buffer latches to zero—at the expense of more complicated sequencing logic. As we recall, the reason for buffering data in and out of the RAM array was to gain bandwidth and therefore reduce the period of time between memory cycles. Since it is impossible to cycle pixel data one by one in and out of memory at video rates and still allow external access cycles, the buffering technique allowed the accumulation of pixel data to then be

- 16,384 X 4 Organization
- Single +5 V Supply (10% Tolerance)
- Performance Ranges:

	ACCESS TIME ROW ADDRESS (MAX)	ACCESS TIME COLUMN ADDRESS (MAX)	READ OR WRITE CYCLE (MIN)	READ, MODIFY, WRITE CYCLE (MIN)
TMS 4416-15	150 ns	80 ns	260 ns	360 ns
TMS 4416-20	200 ns	120 ns	330 ns	460 ns

- Long Refresh Period . . . 4 milliseconds
- Low Refresh Overhead Time . . . As Low As 1.7% of Total Refresh Period
- All Inputs, Outputs, Clocks Fully TTL Compatible
- 3-State Unlatched Outputs
- Early Write or $\overline{G}$ to Control Output Buffer Impedance
- Page-mode Operation for Faster Access
- Low Power Dissipation
  - Operating . . . 130 mW (typ)
  - Standby . . . 17.5 mW (typ.)
- New SMOS (Scaled-MOS) N-Channel Technology

18-PIN PLASTIC DUAL-IN-LINE PACKAGE (TOP VIEW)

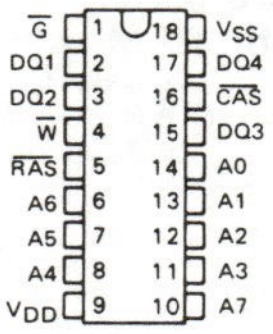

```
        ____
  G   [ 1  18 ] VSS
 DQ1  [ 2   17 ] DQ4
 DQ2  [ 3   16 ] CAS
  W   [ 4   15 ] DQ3
 RAS  [ 5   14 ] A0
  A6  [ 6   13 ] A1
  A5  [ 7   12 ] A2
  A4  [ 8   11 ] A3
 VDD  [ 9   10 ] A7
```

PIN NOMENCLATURE	
A0-A7	Address Inputs
$\overline{CAS}$	Column Address Strobe
DQ1-DQ4	Data In/Data Out
$\overline{G}$	Output Enable
$\overline{RAS}$	Row Address Strobe
$\overline{W}$	Write Enable
VDD	+5 V Supply
VSS	Ground

description

The TMS 4416 NL is a high speed, 65,536-bit, dynamic, random-access memory, organized as 16,384 words of 4 bits each. It employs state-of-the-art SMOS (scaled MOS) N-channel double-level polysilicon gate technology for very high performance combined with low cost and improved reliability.

The TMS 4416 NL features $\overline{RAS}$ access times to 150 ns maximum. Power dissipation is 125 mW typical operating, 17.5 mW typical standby.

New SMOS technology permits operation from a single +5 V supply, reducing system power supply and decoupling requirements, and easing board layout. I_{DD} peaks have been reduced to 60 mA typical, and a −1 V input voltage undershoot can be tolerated, minimizing system noise considerations. Input clamp diodes are used to ease system design.

Refresh period is extended to 4 milliseconds, and during this period each of the 256 rows must be strobed with $\overline{RAS}$ in order to retain data. $\overline{CAS}$ can remain high during the refresh sequence to conserve power.

All inputs and outputs, including clocks, are compatible with Series 74 TTL. All address lines and data-in are latched on chip to simplify system design. Data-out is unlatched to allow greater system flexibility.

The TMS 4416 NL is offered in an 18-pin dual-in-line plastic package and is guaranteed for operation from 0°C to 70°C. Packages are designed for insertion in mounting-hole rows on 300 mil (7.62mm) centers.

Figure 6-15 Typical 16K × 4-bit Dynamic RAM. (Reprinted by permission of Texas Instruments Incorporated, copyright © 1982.)

ADVANCE INFORMATION
This document contains information on a new product. Specifications are subject to change without notice.

TEXAS INSTRUMENTS
INCORPORATED
POST OFFICE BOX 225012 • DALLAS, TEXAS 75265

cycled in larger chunks and slower rates. In the original scheme, all memories in the array are cycled synchronously, meaning that they all carry out the same cycle at the same time. If we think of breaking up the 32-bit wide memory array into four individual pixel-sized banks, we may then sequence pixels in and out of their respective RAM banks in a phased memory cycle scheme. What this means is that now instead of feeding $\overline{RAS}$, $\overline{CAS}$, and $\overline{WE}$ to all RAMs, different time-delayed versions of the signals are sent to the four banks in such a way that they are cycling out of phase with one another. The cycle for the first bank of 16K × 8-bit RAM is started. A quarter of the way through, the second array's cycle starts and so on. As the forth bank completes its cycle, the first bank begins again. The overall cycle time and characteristics for any one bank is still the same as originally described. The key is that as pixels become available from the A/D, every

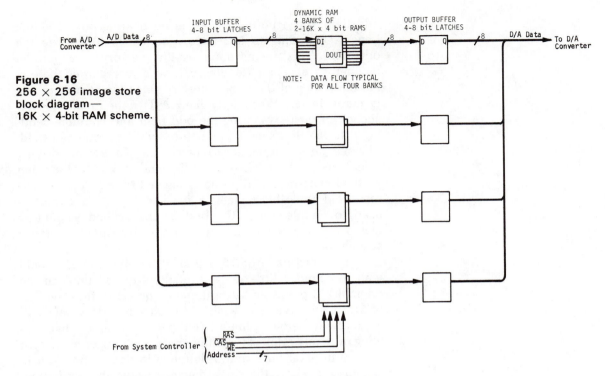

Figure 6-16
256 × 256 image store
block diagram—
16K × 4-bit RAM scheme.

154.1nS, or quarter memory cycle, one bank is at the appropriate point in its cycle to read out data to the D/A and subsequently accept the data from the A/D. As far as the RAMs are concerned, everything is just as it was previously; we have simply skewed the time in which each of the four banks actually executes the various operations within the cycle.

The tradeoff in implementing this new scheme is in the generation of the four phased versions of the various signals needed to drive the RAMs. Instead of single $\overline{RAS}$, $\overline{CAS}$, and $\overline{WE}$ lines, we now need four of each. Additionally, certain other signals for controlling RAM addresses must be generated in a four-phase manner and, subsequently, the external input/output accesses become not as straightforward. All in all, though, from a design complexity and hardware component standpoint, the tradeoffs are tightly competitive.

We now have obtained a compact image store design capable of storing 256 × 256 × 8 bit images. Moving into the 512 × 512 image domain requires only an extension of the methods already covered. The most troublesome aspect in making the jump is that pixel times are only half as long as in the 256-pixel-per-line case. The proper image store design, however, reduces this concern to a minimum.

In attacking the design of the 512 × 512 image store, there are a few items that help to resolve the differences between the previously handled 256 × 256 case and the new job. In the case of the 256-line image store, we recall that digitizing occurred only during one field of the video frame. We will assume that this was the even field. The

97

odd field was ignored as having no bearing on a 256-line image. Upgrading to 512 lines requires us to digitize the odd field. This means doubling the memory in a parallel manner to accept data where it was disregarded before. All the timing of the image store remains the same; nothing is made faster. We simply feed A/D data to the second section of memory during the odd field and continue sending it to the first section, as before, while in the even field. The second set of memory receives all of the same driving signals as the first. The only difference now is that at each vertical sync time, a flip-flop is toggled to indicate the current field that the system is in. The flip-flop's output is used to enable either the first or the second section of memory. Enhancing the system to 512 lines is fairly straightforward.

The upgrade from 256 pixels per line to 512 would tend to sound a little more difficult. We may think of the original 256 pixels as being the even pixels in the new line of 512 pixels. We now wish to include the odd pixels falling halfway between the original pixel locations. This doubling of pixels implies three things—a doubling of memory, a halving in pixel time, and a doubling in data bandwidth to memory, to allow the same memory cycle time as before. These three implications are all interrelated. If we double memory, we must do so in such a way as to double the bandwidth at the same time. This in turn takes care of the problem of pixels coming twice as fast. This is accomplished by the addition of four new banks of RAM in between the previous four banks found in the 256-pixel-per-line version. The original four banks store the even pixels as before, while the new banks store the odd pixels. Figure 6-17 illustrates the complete 512 × 512 image store design.

In the data buffering technique, the number of buffers must be increased by a factor of two. We will now be buffering pixels into 8-pixel chunks to achieve the originally required RAM cycle time—8 pixels × 77.03nS pixel time = 616.4nS. If we are to use the scheme of phased memory cycling, we will require eight phases of the memory driving signals. As before, each time a pixel is available from the A/D (now every 77.04nS), one of the eight RAM banks will be at the point in its cycle to read out a pixel to the D/A and then accept the pixel from the A/D.

All in all, we have increased the capacity of the image store by expanding on the design techniques used to develop the original 256 × 256 store. Even though pixels are coming twice as fast, the slower RAM cycle time requirements remain preserved.

The high point of this 512 × 512 design is that it may be reduced in size to 512 × 256, 256 × 512, or 256 × 256 simply by removing RAM chips. The same design accommodates all four image size formats and may be configured as required by a given application. A 256 line × 512 pixel image store is made by removing one field section of RAM

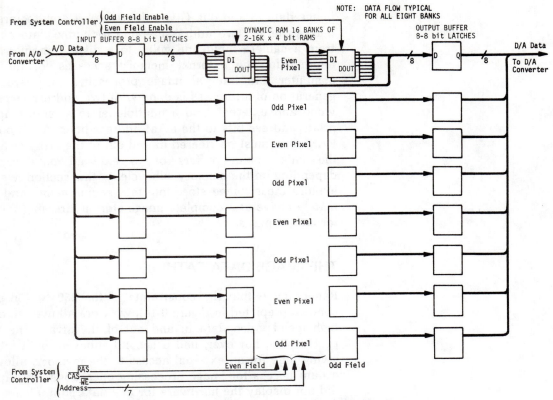

Figure 6-17 512 × 512 image store block diagram — 16K × 4-bit RAM scheme.

so that only a single field of the video frame is stored. A 512 line by 256 pixel store is made by pulling every other bank of RAM within both field sections, allowing only every other pixel in a 512-pixel line to be stored. Of course, a 256 line × 256 pixel store is handled by carrying out both of the above RAM extractions, reducing the store to an identical state as that in the original 256 × 256 store design.

As newer dynamic RAM chips become available, the physical size of an image store can become smaller. For instance, a 32K × 4-bit RAM could replace two RAM chips in the 512 × 512 store design by merging both fields of image data to reside in the same chip. As long as data bandwidth is maintained, virtually any RAM architecture improvement may be implemented.

We now have a means to capture, store, and display image data. The remaining task is to effectively sequence data in and out of the image store during the external access cycle to allow simultaneous image processing. Along with internal image processing hardware, to be discussed in Chapter 7, the system will be complete.

Stored Image Interface

Having an image store with the capacity of a full video frame, whether 256 × 256, 512 × 512, or another, leaves us with the necessity of RAM array addressing for sequencing

99

image data in and out. Given the two-port architecture, we must generate two addresses—one for video data coming from a camera input and going to a display monitor, and another for the external memory accesses for the host computer and internal image processing hardware. The generation of addresses is done with two address counters, video and external, and a multiplexer to steer the appropriate address bits to the RAM address lines. Additionally, RAM data must be steered in and out of the array to either the video pixel buffers or to external data latches, depending on the memory subcycle. In this section, we will explore these image store interface requirements and ultimately arrive at a complete image store addressing scheme for our purposes.

THE IMAGE DATA PATH

Remaining within the constraints of the 256 × 256 store concept (depicted in Figure 6-16), we were allowed to cycle high-speed video data in and out of the array. The two-port design, however, had a second subcycle built into it, giving time for an external access to the memory, allowing a data access for image processing operations. This figure did not display the hardware for this data path. Figure 6-18 illustrates a more complex view. Four external input and output buffers have been added, feeding external data into and out of the RAM array. During the internal video

Figure 6-18 256 × 256 image store block diagram—16K × 4-bit RAM scheme with external input/output buffers.

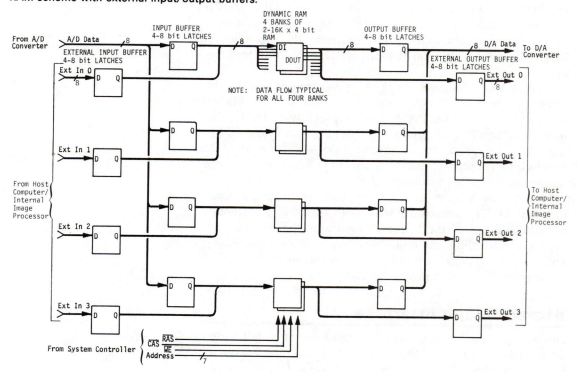

input/output subcycle, pixel data proceed as discussed before. While in the external subcycle, data flows through the external buffer latches to or from the host computer or internal image processing hardware. The external buffer latches accommodate four-pixel read or writes during the external subcycle. During any external cycle, the four pixels accessed are sequential, since they come simultaneously from the four banks of RAM. Therefore, the external cycle allows random data from cycle to cycle but the four pixels accessed in any one cycle are sequential pixel locations within the video frame. As will be discussed in the next chapter, the image processing hardware may buffer groups of four pixels, allowing several processes to occur before writing data back to an image store.

SEQUENCING IMAGE DATA
IN AND OUT OF MEMORY

Addressing of the image store is handled by four counter elements—two for the video input/output subcycle and two for the external input/output subcycle. Each subcycle's counters are composed of a pixel counter and a line counter. By steering the correct address counter bits to the RAM array at the right time, image data are accessed in an orderly manner, allowing the flow to be in harmony with the rest of the system. Figure 6-19 illustrates the counter arrangement. Looking at the video address counters first, we see two 8-bit counters. The first 8-bit counter keeps track of the video pixel address, pixel 0 to 255. The two low-order bits are used to control loading of pixel data from the A/D to the four input buffers and from the output buffers to the D/A. The high-order 6-bits go the RAM and form the first six bits of the 7-bit row address. Since four pixels are read and written to RAM at the same time, it makes sense that the least significant row address to the RAM array would be the third bit in the pixel address. The first two bits represent one of four pixels within any four-pixel RAM word; remember, the RAM data width is 32 bits, or four pixels.

The second 8-bit counter is the line counter representing the current line of the video data from 0 to 255. The least significant bit becomes the seventh bit of the RAM row address while the seven most significant bits comprise the RAM column address bits. From this we see that 16 bits of address information fully describes the location of one pixel in the image frame of 65,536 pixels. Fourteen bits locate a block of four pixels within the RAM array and the other two bits decode which of the four is to come into or out of the pixel buffers at any given time. The video address counters are incremented (or clocked), once every pixel time, addressing the next location for the current pixel to reside.

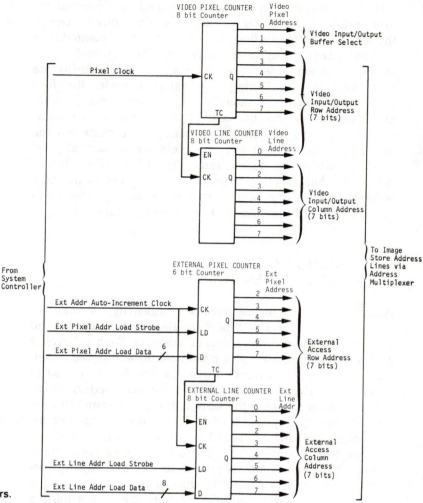

Figures 6-19 Image store address counters.

The external address counters work exactly like the video address counters as far as the definitions of their bits. There are two differences, though. The first is that the pixel counter is only six bits, rather than eight as the video address counter was. These six bits represent the six high-order address lines. While the two low-order bits of the video address counters controlled the steering of pixel data into and out of the four buffer latches, this is not the case in the external access mode. Every time we do an external access we either read or write four pixels at a time. Since the internal image processing hardware is running at a fast pace, it is in our interest to transfer as much information to and from the image store as possible during each given access subcycle. Because of the four-pixel buffering scheme adopted earlier in the image store design, we are inherently given access to four sequential pixels every time an image store access is made. Therefore, it makes sense for us to process all four pixels before writing the resulting pixel data back to the image store.

The second difference associated with the external access address counters is that they may be preloaded

102

with an address to be accessed. This preloading is done by the host computer or internal image processing hardware, depending on what data either device may wish to access in the upcoming external access subcycle. With the loading of the external address counters, a new chunk of four pixels may be accessed from the image store once every 616.4nS. This access may, of course, be either a Read or a Write.

In Chapter 7, we will discuss in depth the hardware implementation of pixel point and group processing of images. The speed at which this hardware operates as well as how fast and efficiently data may be accessed to and from the image store, is critical. Because of their common use, image store address sequencing plays an important role in these processes. General frame processing also requires address sequencing. However, these processes vary to such degrees that, for a given application, address sequencing becomes very specialized. These processes are usually left up to the host computer to carry out. For these reasons, frame process address sequencing will not be discussed here.

For a pixel point process, every pixel in the image frame is operated upon using a mapping function. There is no regard paid in the operation to spatial location of a given pixel or its neighboring pixels. To carry out the pixel point operation, the image processing hardware need only read a pixel block-of-four, map their values into output values, and write the results back into an image store. The resulting values may be written back to the original input image store or to another, if present in the system. In either case, the image store that receives processed data is called the output image store. Addressing of image data for this operation is simple: we start at line 0, pixel 0 and finish at line 255, pixel 255. Rather than requiring the image processor to load a new pixel address to the external address counters prior to each access, it makes sense to add an automatic-incrementing circuit. Following each access by the image processor, the counters may then increment to the next block-of-four pixel address automatically. This auto-incrementing feature may be further enhanced so that it has the options, under host computer or internal image processor control, of increment-on-read, increment-on-write, increment-on-read-and-write, or no increment at all. Additional capabilities will be nice to add later as we consider pixel group processing.

To perform a single image point process, the image processor initializes the external address counter to line 0, pixel 0 and sets the increment mode to increment-on-write. In the first access cycle, it reads the image store external data buffers. This first read is four pixels wide and represents line 0, pixels 0, 1, 2, and 3. The mapping function is applied to the four pixels. The point process cycle on the first four pixels is completed by writing the four pixels back to the output image store. Since auto-incrementing is in the increment-on-write mode, the results are written back to the same locations as where read. At the end of the write cycle, the address increment is automatically performed and the external address counter is pointing to the next location in the image store. The image processor continues as before until the entire image is processed.

Of interest here is whether the image processor can actually process the four pixels in time to stick the results back in the image store the following external access cycle, 616.1nS later. It turns out, as we will see in Chapter 7, that this is easily accomplished. So given that it takes two external access cycles to process four pixels, our final time to complete a pixel point operation on a full image frame is 616.1nS external access cycle time $\times$ 2 cycles $\times$ (256 $\times$ 256 pixels/4 pixels per operation) = 20.19mS. This boils down to being considerably less than one video frame time of 33.33mS.

The dual image pixel point process case is similar to the single image case. All the addressing remains the same. As the image processor does the read, two image stores respond with their respective pixel data simultaneously. The processor must then operate on the four pixel pairs and return the results to the output image store. The processing time remains the same as for a single image operation, 20.19mS.

Pixel group processing becomes a bit more troublesome, as we would expect, due to its more complicated nature. As we recall, the calculation for one output pixel value is composed of nine multiplications followed by nine additions. This means that nine pixels must be accessed from the image store before a single pixel calculation may be made. The resulting value must then be written back to the output image store. Keep in mind, though, that of the nine pixels used in a calculation, six will be used in the following calculation. Additionally, the subsequent calculation will use three of the original nine pixels. Figure 6-20 illustrates this pixel accessing. It behooves us to save accessed pixels until they have been used to their fullest extent, thereby reducing the number of times that the image store must be accessed. To see how this works, we first remember that each access to the image store yields four sequential pixels in a given line.

To understand the access methods for efficient group processing, let us jump into the middle of a line being processed (see Figure 6-21). We have just completed the calculations for the arbitrarily named pixels *o*, *p*, and *q*. In order to calculate the result for *r*, however, it is necessary to read in the next three blocks of four pixels. Now we may calculate *r*, giving us the block of four, *o*, *p*, *q* and *r*, to be written to the output image store. With the six blocks of four pixels currently stored and in use by the image processing hardware, *s*, *t*, and *u* may also be calculated. We

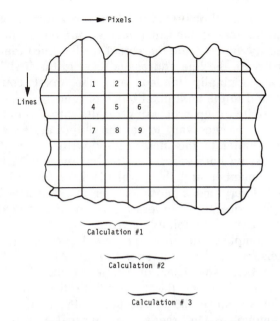

Calculation #1

Calculation #2

Calculation # 3

Figure 6-20 Any subsequent group process calculation will use 6 input pixels from the previous calculation.

note, though, that once *t* is calculated, the three blocks to the left are no longer needed. While *u* is being calculated, the hardware goes to the image store and retrieves the next three blocks, placing them in the registers holding the blocks no longer needed. The data are now present to calculate *v*, *w*, *x*, and *y*. Once *v* is calculated, *s*, *t*, *u*, and *v* are written to the output image store simultaneously.

As far as addressing to the input store goes, we read three blocks of four pixels from three sequential lines and then increment to the next four-pixel block boundary and read in the next three blocks of four pixels from the same three sequential lines. Adding an additional mode to the auto-increment portion of the external address counters will facilitate faster reading of the image store for pixel group processing, eliminating the need for the address to be updated prior to each read. The new mode works like this: the image processing hardware loads the external address counter with the top-most line number and the pixel block of four to be accessed. Normally, the pixel block to be first used will be block 0, consisting of the first four pixels in the line. The mode is then set to group-increment mode and the reading begins. The first address to be read

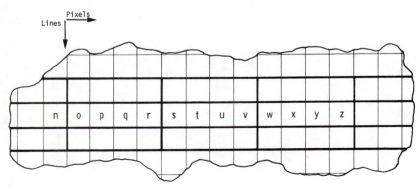

Figure 6-21 The group process image store access sequence.

is the same as that preloaded into the address counters. The line address is then incremented for the second read, followed by another line increment for the third read. After the third read, the line address is reset to the first line address, as originally loaded, and the pixel counter is incremented to the next pixel block of four.

To write group processing results into the output image store, it is necessary to set the output store's external address counter to the increment-on-write mode. The image processing hardware loads the counters with the topmost line number and the pixel block of four to be first accessed. Everytime a block of four pixels are written to the output store, the counters increment to the next block in anticipation of the following write.

To complete the group process for an entire line of 256 pixels, we find it necessary to read 3 lines $\times$ 64 pixel blocks, or 192 reads. Then, of course, 64 pixel block writes are required to store the results into the output image store. For an entire 256 $\times$ 256 image, the total reads and writes amount to (192 reads + 64 writes) $\times$ 256 lines = 65,536 image store accesses. This amounts to an image store input/output time of 65,536 $\times$ 616.1nS = 40.38mS.

Keeping within the arena of low-cost image processing, achieving computational speeds to keep up with the group process input/output time is extremely difficult. The problem is that there are several time-intensive calculations to be completed for each and every output pixel computation. In Chapter 7, we present hardware capable of completing an entire image group process in roughly 150mS, a very reasonable figure for the low-end user.

With the features of auto-incrementing image store external address counters, the job image processing hardware is reduced, helping to speed the overall operations. In the next chapter we will delve into the actual hardware implementations of the processes discussed in Chapter 5.

Image Data Processor 7

The heart of the image processing system is the image processor hardware itself. Its speed in carrying out the commonly used algorithms of interest can be a pacing factor in the time-efficiency of the overall system. In Chapter 6, we discussed the storage of digital images and went into detail about the accessing of pixel information for use by the image processing hardware. This chapter explores the hardware and mechanics associated with the actual processing of digital images. It should be remembered that the concepts presented here are aimed at a low-cost image processing system. Although general in a conceptual context, they are presented here as a guide to the critical factors encountered in basic image processing hardware design.

In Chapters 2 and 5, four classes of image processing were discussed—pixel point/single image, pixel point/dual image, group, and frame. With frame processing as the possible exception, these operations may be carried out in rather simple hardware yielding fast results to the user. Of course, the alternative would be for the host computer to do the processing in software. For many applications, though, the time of calculation by a host computer can be prohibitive. Instead, we handle the basic functions using image processing hardware, giving control to the host machine. This scheme allows common processing to be handled quickly by the image processing system, leaving the more special-purpose processes up to the host computer.

Image processing hardware may be highly complex and costly or simple and low-cost. The basic difference is in its speed of execution. Most commercially available image processing systems utilize a complex approach based on arrays of high-speed video buffers and multiplier chips. The accepted benchmark operation of 3 × 3 group process on an entire image frame is one frame time of 33.33mS. We might question the necessity of this kind of speed for low-end applications. Most users, in fact, can live with much slower times—five or six frame times, for instance. Six frame times is 6 x 33.33mS = 200.0mS. Given this speed, five group processes can be carried out in a second, which is often more than acceptable. Cost reduction is on the order of ten to one between the two approaches.

This chapter pursues the basic design of low-cost image processing hardware, allowing for processing speeds suitable to most applications. For the sake of consistency, we remain within the 256 × 256 image format.

Single Image Pixel Point Processor

The pixel point processor must be configured in such a way that both single and dual image processes may be handled. We will first cover the fundamental implementation of a single image processor. The following section will then configure a composite dual image processor that may default to the single image case.

As discussed in Chapter 5, point processing operates independently on each input image store pixel, generating corresponding output pixels. The general equation is of the form $O[x,y] = M[I(x,y)]$, where $I(x,y)$ represents an input pixel at the coordinates (x,y), $O(x,y)$ represents an output pixel at the coordinates (x,y) and M is the mapping function. The function M takes on the characteristics of a mathematical equation, converting the brightnesses of input pixels to resulting output values. To carry out this operation in hardware, it would seem likely that pixels would be retrieved from the input image store, run through specialized hardware that implements the equation M, and returned to the output store. This process, however, can be time consuming, expensive and, as it turns out, very inefficient. There is an easier and much faster way to handle this process. All pixels, when quantized to eight bits, have, by definition, a brightness value of between 0 and 255. Since the point function, $O(x,y) = M[I(x,y)]$, maps brightness values into new ones, there are only 256 possible map points. Each input value must correspond to one of the 256 defined output values. Instead of running each pixel's brightness through the equation, we may simply use it to drive a *look-up table*, or LUT. Once the 256 values of the LUT are calculated through the mapping function, the point operation is reduced to a simple look-up procedure, greatly reducing processing time. The key here is realizing that no matter how complex the mapping function may be, there are eight bits defining any given pixel's brightness; and, therefore, 256 possible values for the input pixel at (x,y); and, subsequently, only 256 possible values that the output pixel may take on.

The implementation of the LUT in hardware is done by way of a high-speed RAM. The RAM must have a data width of eight bits and a depth of at least 256 locations. To map an input pixel value to an output pixel result, the input pixel drives the eight address lines of the RAM. In response, the RAM places eight bits of data on its output lines corresponding to the addressed location. The eight bits of data become the output pixel result. Given an input pixel of any 8-bit value, from 0 to 255, an 8-bit output value is generated. The data generated by way of the RAM address is dependent on what has been loaded into the RAM by the host computer before the operation. The RAM effectively carries out the mapping function—input pixel brightnesses are mapped to output pixel brightnesses.

As an example of loading a mapping function, let us consider the point operation where all pixels below a brightness of 135 are to be set to black, or 0, and all pixels with a brightness of 135 or higher set to white, or 255. The process, discussed earlier, is called binary contrast enhancement. Figure 7-1 shows the mapping function. To load this map into the RAM, we sequentially address RAM locations beginning with location 0. At location 0, we write the 8-bit data corresponding to the desired output pixel brightness, given an input pixel brightness of 0. The data written is a 0 as defined by the mapping function. Next, location 1 is written with a 0, and so on through location 134. At location 135, our equation calls for a brightness of 255 to be the resulting output for an input brightness of 135. 255 is written into location 135. Locations 136 through 255 are similarly loaded with the data 255. The RAM now contains the appropriate map to implement the defined point operation.

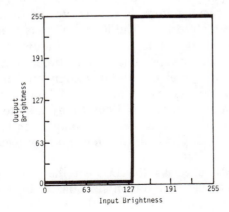

Figure 7-1 A typical pixel point process map used for binary contrast enhancement.

The hardware involved in implementing pixel point processing on a stored image is not difficult to realize. As discussed in Chapter 6, all Read and Write accesses to an image store are carried out in four-pixel chunks. Once four pixels have been read from the input image store, their values reside in the image store external output buffers. The latched pixel data subsequently feeds the point processor hardware. One by one, the point processor sequences through the four pixels. Each is allowed to drive the LUT's address lines with the output data results being latched into the point processor output buffers. Once all four pixels have been processed, the results are written back to the output image store.

Figure 7-2 illustrates the single image point processor. The host computer is responsible for loading the LUT with the required look-up data prior to an operation. This loading is accomplished by suspending the LUT input drivers while the host computer drives the address, data in, and write enable lines. The data path between the host computer and LUT has been omitted from the figure for clarity.

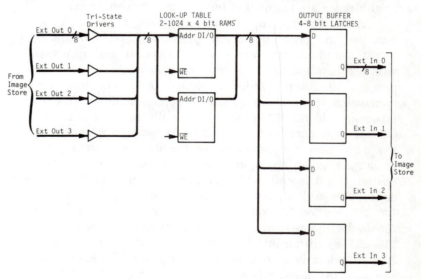

Figure 7-2 Pixel point/single image processor hardware.

The timing involved in the point processor is that of a four-state sequencer. First pixel 0, of the four pixels read from the input image store, is enabled to the RAM address lines via a tri-state driver. The RAM result is then clocked into output latch 0. Pixels 1, 2, and 3 follow in a similar manner. In order to yield a fast point processor, we wish to have the four pixel calculations completed in time for the next allowed access to the output image store. This sets 616.1nS as the maximum time it may take to complete the process. This timing is met by making each look-up cycle occur in 150nS, giving a total four-pixel processing time of 600nS.

The RAM used as the LUT in the point processor must be at least 256 × 8 bits in size. Basically, a variety of RAM chips may be chosen to do the job; we will use two

1K × 4-bit RAMs because they are widely available. A suitable 1K × 4-bit chip is the Intel 2148H-2, having an access time of 45nS (see Figure 7-3). Summing the 45nS RAM access time with the propagation times for the data to flow through the input tri-state drivers and set up at the inputs of the output latches, we find the 150nS processing cycle time is accommodated with no problem.

intel®

2148H
1024 x 4 BIT STATIC RAM

	2148H-2	2148H-3	2148H	2148HL-3	2148HL
Max. Access Time (ns)	45	55	70	55	70
Max. Active Current (mA)	180	180	180	125	125
Max. Standby Current (mA)	30	30	30	20	20

- **Automatic Power-Down**
- **Industry Standard 2114A and 2148 Pinout**
- **HMOS II Technology**
- **Functionally Compatible to the 2148**
- **Completely Static Memory — No Clock or Timing Strobe Required**
- **Equal Access and Cycle Times**
- **High Density 18-Pin Package**
- **Common Data Input and Output**
- **Three-State Output**
- **Single +5V Supply**
- **Fast Chip Select Access 2149H Available**

The Intel® 2148H is a 4096-bit static Random Access Memory organized as 1024 words by 4 bits using HMOS II, a high-performance MOS technology. It uses a uniquely innovative design approach which provides the ease-of-use features associated with non-clocked static memories and the reduced standby power dissipation associated with clocked static memories. To the user this means low standby power dissipation without the need for clocks, address setup and hold times, nor reduced data rates due to cycle times that are longer than access times.

$\overline{CS}$ controls the power-down feature. In less than a cycle time after $\overline{CS}$ goes high — disabling the 2148H — the part automatically reduces its power requirements and remains in this low power standby mode as long as $\overline{CS}$ remains high. This device feature results in system power savings as great as 85% in larger systems, where the majority of devices are disabled. A non-power-down companion, the 2149H, is available to provide a fast chip select access time for speed critical applications.

The 2148H is assembled in an 18-pin package configured with the industry standard 1K x 4 pinout. It is directly TTL compatible in all respects: inputs, outputs, and a single +5V supply. The data is read out nondestructively and has the same polarity as the input data.

PIN NAMES

A_0-A_9	ADDRESS INPUTS
$\overline{WE}$	WRITE ENABLE
$\overline{CS}$	CHIP SELECT
I/O_1-I/O_4	DATA INPUT/OUTPUT
V_{CC}	POWER (+5V)
GND	GROUND

TRUTH TABLE

$\overline{CS}$	$\overline{WE}$	MODE	I/O	POWER
H	X	NOT SELECTED	HIGH-Z	STANDBY
L	L	WRITE	D_{IN}	ACTIVE
L	H	READ	D_{OUT}	ACTIVE

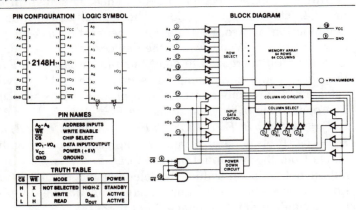

Figure 1. Pin Configuration, Logic Symbol, Pin Names and Truth Table

Figure 2. 2148H Block Diagram

Figure 7-3 Typical 1K × 4-bit Static RAM. (Reprinted by permission of Intel Corporation, copyright © 1980.)

The basic point process cycle requires an external read access from the input image store followed by an external write access to the output image store in order to process four pixels. The image store external access address counters are set in the increment-on-write auto-increment mode, thus forcing the counters to step to the next four-pixel block following a write to the output store. As far as the point processor is concerned, image store addressing is totally autonomous. Therefore, an entire 256 × 256 image may be processed in 2 accesses × 616.1nS per access $\times$ 64 blocks of 4 pixels per line $\times$ 256 lines = 20.19mS. This is less than one frame time, and appears to be instantaneous to the user.

Dual Image Point Processor

Implementing the dual image point processor in hardware requires an expansion of the described single image circuit. Expanding the design to handle two image pixel data paths as input requires the addition of an input port and associated LUT. Furthermore, to accommodate the combination of any two given pixels we add an *Arithmetic Logic Unit,* or ALU. Following the ALU, an output LUT is added to accommodate arithmetic overflow conditions. These enhancements to the original single image design give the capability to do dual image point processing while retaining the single image processing capability.

As in the single image circuit, we want four pixels to be processed in one external image store access cycle time of 616.1nS. Therefore, the per-pixel processing time remains at 150nS. The addition of an ALU and output LUT will add on the order of 30nS and 45nS, respectively, to the existing 45nS input LUT access time. Including propagation times for the data to pass through the input tri-state drivers and set up on the output latch inputs, we are still able to meet the 150nS time.

The ALU used in this design is composed of a pair of 74S181 type chips; the specification sheet is shown in Figure 7-4. This ALU chip allows the logical and arithmetic combination of two 4-bit numbers, generating a 4-bit plus carry bit result. When two of the devices are cascaded, the data length is increased to eight bits plus a carry bit. Function, mode, and carry input lines drive the ALU, allowing selection of a number of combination operations to occur. The operations of interest to us are $F = A + B$, $F = A - B$, $F = A$ AND B, $F = A$ OR B, $F = A$ XOR B, $F = A$, and $F = $ NOT A; where A and B represent corresponding pixels from the two input image stores, and F is the combination output pixel value. By selecting the required function we are able to combine images on a pixel-by-pixel basis, yielding the dual image point process.

Figure 7-5 illustrates the point processor capable of executing single and dual image operations. The combination select inputs to the ALU are under control of the host computer along with the capability of loading the three LUTs. Again, the loading of the LUTs by the host computer is implied and has not been included in the illustration for the sake of clarity. The processing cycle of data from the two input image stores to the output store is identical to that described for the single image point processor. The processing time for a complete image frame of 256×256 remains at 20.19mS.

TTL
MSI

TYPES SN54181, SN54LS181, SN54S181, SN74181, SN74LS181, SN74S181
ARITHMETIC LOGIC UNITS/FUNCTION GENERATORS
BULLETIN NO. DL-S 7611831, DECEMBER 1972 — REVISED OCTOBER 1976

SN54181, SN54LS181, SN54S181 . . . J OR W PACKAGE
SN74181, SN74LS181, SN74S181 . . . J OR N PACKAGE
(TOP VIEW)

logic: see tables 1 and 2

- Full Look-Ahead for High-Speed Operations on Long Words
- Input Clamping Diodes Minimize Transmission-Line Effects
- Darlington Outputs Reduce Turn-Off Time
- Arithmetic Operating Modes:
  - Addition
  - Subtraction
  - Shift Operand A One Position
  - Magnitude Comparison
  - Plus Twelve Other Arithmetic Operations
- Logic Function Modes:
  - Exclusive-OR
  - Comparator
  - AND, NAND, OR, NOR
  - Plus Ten Other Logic Operations

TYPICAL ADDITION TIMES

NUMBER OF BITS	ADDITION TIMES USING 'LS181 AND '182	USING '181 AND '182	USING 'S181 AND 'S182	USING 'LS181	PACKAGE COUNT ARITHMETIC/ LOGIC UNITS	LOOK-AHEAD CARRY GENERATORS	CARRY METHOD BETWEEN ALU's
1 to 4	24 ns	24 ns	11 ns		1		NONE
5 to 8	36 ns	40 ns	18 ns		2		RIPPLE
9 to 16	36 ns	44 ns	19 ns		3 or 4	1	FULL LOOK-AHEAD
17 to 64	60 ns	68 ns	28 ns		5 to 16	2 to 5	FULL LOOK-AHEAD

description

The '181, 'LS181, and 'S181 are arithmetic logic units (ALU)/function generators that have a complexity of 75 equivalent gates on a monolithic chip. These circuits perform 16 binary arithmetic operations on two 4-bit words as shown in Tables 1 and 2. These operations are selected by the four function-select lines (S0, S1, S2, S3) and include addition, subtraction, decrement, and straight transfer. When performing arithmetic manipulations, the internal carries must be enabled by applying a low-level voltage to the mode control input (M). A full carry look-ahead scheme is made available in these devices for fast, simultaneous carry generation by means of two cascade-outputs (pins 15 and 17) for the four bits in the package. When used in conjunction with the SN54182, SN54S182, or SN74S182, full carry look-ahead circuits, high-speed arithmetic operations can be performed. The typical addition times shown above illustrate the little additional time required for addition of longer words when full carry look-ahead is employed. The method of cascading '182 or 'S182 circuits with these ALU's to provide multi-level full carry look-ahead is illustrated under typical applications data for the '182 and 'S182.

If high speed is not of importance, a ripple-carry input (C_n) and a ripple-carry output (C_{n+4}) are available. However, the ripple-carry delay has also been minimized so that arithmetic manipulations for small word lengths can be performed without external circuitry.

TABLE 1

SELECTION				M = H LOGIC FUNCTIONS	M = L ARITHMETIC OPERATIONS	
S3	S2	S1	S0		C_n = L (no carry)	C_n = H (with carry)
L	L	L	L	F = $\overline{A}$	F = A MINUS 1	F = A
L	L	L	H	F = $\overline{A\overline{B}}$	F = AB MINUS 1	F = AB
L	L	H	L	F = $\overline{A} + B$	F = A$\overline{B}$ MINUS 1	F = A$\overline{B}$
L	L	H	H	F = 1	F = MINUS 1 (2's COMPL)	F = ZERO
L	H	L	L	F = $\overline{A + B}$	F = A PLUS (A + $\overline{B}$)	F = A PLUS A$\overline{B}$
L	H	L	H	F = $\overline{B}$	F = AB PLUS (A + $\overline{B}$)	F = AB PLUS A$\overline{B}$
L	H	H	L	F = $\overline{A \oplus B}$	F = A MINUS B MINUS 1	F = A MINUS B
L	H	H	H	F = A + $\overline{B}$	F = A + $\overline{B}$	F = (A + $\overline{B}$) PLUS 1
H	L	L	L	F = $\overline{A}B$	F = A PLUS (A + B)	F = A PLUS AB
H	L	L	H	F = A $\oplus$ B	F = A PLUS B	F = A PLUS B PLUS 1
H	L	H	L	F = B	F = A$\overline{B}$ PLUS (A + B)	F = A$\overline{B}$ PLUS (A + B) PLUS 1
H	L	H	H	F = A + B	F = (A + B)	F = (A + B) PLUS 1
H	H	L	L	F = 0	F = A PLUS A*	F = A PLUS A PLUS 1
H	H	L	H	F = A$\overline{B}$	F = AB PLUS A	F = AB PLUS A PLUS 1
H	H	H	L	F = AB	F = A$\overline{B}$ PLUS A	F = A$\overline{B}$ PLUS A PLUS 1
H	H	H	H	F = A	F = A	F = A PLUS 1

TABLE 2

SELECTION				M = H LOGIC FUNCTIONS	M = L ARITHMETIC OPERATIONS	
S3	S2	S1	S0		$\overline{C}_n$ = H (no carry)	$\overline{C}_n$ = L (with carry)
L	L	L	L	F = $\overline{A}$	F = A	F = A PLUS 1
L	L	L	H	F = $\overline{A + B}$	F = A + B	F = (A + B) PLUS 1
L	L	H	L	F = $\overline{A}B$	F = A + $\overline{B}$	F = (A + $\overline{B}$) PLUS 1
L	L	H	H	F = 0	F = MINUS 1 (2's COMPL)	F = ZERO
L	H	L	L	F = $\overline{AB}$	F = A PLUS A$\overline{B}$	F = A PLUS A$\overline{B}$ PLUS 1
L	H	L	H	F = $\overline{B}$	F = (A + B) PLUS A$\overline{B}$	F = (A + B) PLUS A$\overline{B}$ PLUS 1
L	H	H	L	F = A $\oplus$ B	F = A MINUS B MINUS 1	F = A MINUS B
L	H	H	H	F = A$\overline{B}$	F = A$\overline{B}$ MINUS 1	F = A$\overline{B}$
H	L	L	L	F = $\overline{A} + B$	F = A PLUS AB	F = A PLUS AB PLUS 1
H	L	L	H	F = A $\oplus$ B	F = A PLUS B	F = A PLUS B PLUS 1
H	L	H	L	F = B	F = (A + $\overline{B}$) PLUS AB	F = (A + $\overline{B}$) PLUS AB PLUS 1
H	L	H	H	F = AB	F = AB MINUS 1	F = AB
H	H	L	L	F = 1	F = A PLUS A*	F = A PLUS A PLUS 1
H	H	L	H	F = A + $\overline{B}$	F = (A + B) PLUS A	F = (A + B) PLUS A PLUS 1
H	H	H	L	F = A + B	F = (A + $\overline{B}$) PLUS A	F = (A + $\overline{B}$) PLUS A PLUS 1
H	H	H	H	F = A	F = A MINUS 1	F = A

*Each bit is shifted to the next more significant position.

TEXAS INSTRUMENTS
INCORPORATED
POST OFFICE BOX 5012 • DALLAS, TEXAS 75222

Figure 7-4 74S181 arithmetic logic unit. (Reprinted by permission of Texas Instruments Incorporated, copyright, © 1981.)

113

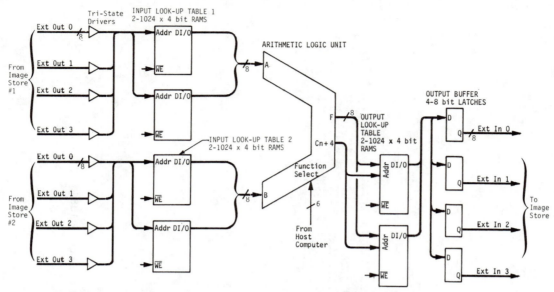

Figure 7-5 Pixel point/dual image processor hardware.

Combined pixel data present at the output of the ALU proceeds to drive the address lines of the output LUT. When implementing logical combinations such as AND, OR, XOR, and NOT, there will have been no carry information generated. In these cases, the output LUT may be simply loaded with a one-to-one map so that the same data that goes in from the ALU appears at the LUT output. In carrying out additions or subtractions, however, carry information is generated out of the ALU. This carry bit must be used by the LUT to reconform the final point processed data into a valid 8-bit pixel format.

In the case of addition, adding two pixels may yield a number out of the 8-bit output range. For instance, adding two 8-bit pixels of value 255 each, yields a result of 510, out of the range for a valid 8-bit pixel. To preclude this type of overflow condition from happening during a dual image add operation, we must load a divide-by-two scaling map into the output LUT (see Figure 7-6). This means that the resulting 512 level gray scale is reduced to a 256 level scale. Now when two pixels are added, the maximum value will be 255 as a result of adding two pixels of brightness 255. Our end product in the add is a valid 8-bit pixel with no opportunity for overflow.

When doing an image subtraction, the process may yield a negative number. Generally, it is implied that when subtracting two pixels we actually wish to have the absolute difference between the two values. If the pixel being subtracted from is larger than the second pixel, the result will be positive and considered an acceptable output quantity. However, if the pixel being subtracted from is smaller than the second pixel, the result will be negative. For example, if a pixel of brightness 246 is subtracted from one of brightness 128, the result will be −118. The end value to be generated by the point processor should be the absolute

114

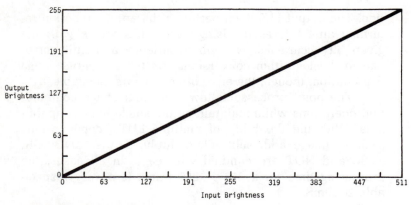

Figure 7-6 Divide by 2 output LUT map.

Figure 7-7 Absolute value output LUT map.

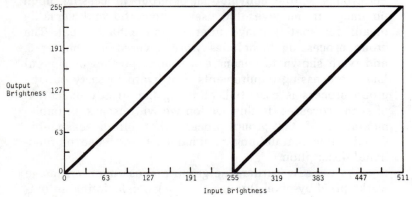

difference, or |128 − 246| = 118. To insure this, the LUT must be loaded in such a way that a one-to-one map is implemented for the eight data bits from the ALU regardless of the state of the carry bit. This LUT map is shown in Figure 7-7.

To make the point processor operate in the single image mode, we simply select the ALU function F = A and load the first LUT with the desired map. The pixel in process will flow through the LUT, being modified by the look-up map and then pass right through the ALU untouched to the appropriate output latch.

Two combination functions of interest have not yet been covered; dual image multiplication and division. One way of handling these operations with the hardware as described is to use the method of adding and subtracting the logarithms of the two pixels being operated upon. The equivalent operation to multiplying two numbers is to take the logs of the numbers, add them and perform an antilog on the result. Division is identical, except that the two logs are subtracted. The logarithm conversion may be implemented using the input LUTs loaded with a log mapping function and the output LUT loaded with an antilog mapping function. The ALU then adds or subtracts, yielding a result that is the log of the multiplication or division opera-

115

tion. The output LUT then performs the antilog function returning an 8-bit result. Using base-2 logarithms with the given bit accuracies, we will experience a definite error due to the logarithm conversions. As far as visible image degradation, though, the error often appears negligible.

The point processor allows full dual image combination operations while maintaining the single image capabilities. With the flexibility of multiple LUTs, combinations such as image add, subtract, multiply, divide, AND, OR, XOR, and NOT are handled with ease. In all cases, the processing time for a 256 × 256 frame is a very respectable 20.19mS.

Pixel Group Processor

Performing spatial convolution, or group processing, upon an image frame gives the user a powerful and versatile means for spatial image filtering and enhancement. The group processing techniques were covered in Chapter 5, and were shown to encompass a large portion of general image processing requirements. Hardware to carry out the group process is essential, allowing the speedy execution of such processes. In this section we will discuss an implementation of the group process that offers reasonable speed while maintaining minimal cost and ease of functional description.

As we saw earlier, the group process upon an image works pixel-by-pixel through the image, calculating an output pixel value based on a weighted average of the input pixel value and its eight neighbors. The nine weighting coefficients remain constant throughout the entire processing of a given image frame. The calculation of an output pixel requires multiplying the input pixel and its eight neighbors by the respective nine weighting coefficients and summing the products. Therefore, for a 256 × 256 image this sequence must be done 256 × 256 = 65,536 times.

Two basic data buffers exist in the group processor: a pixel data buffer and a convolution coefficient data buffer. As discussed in Chapter 6, pixel data are read from the input store in blocks of four. Additionally, the auto-increment mode of the input image store external access address counter is set to increment-for-group-processing. As the input store is read by the group processor, pixel blocks will come sequentially from three consecutive image lines, in groups of four, providing the necessary neighborhood pixel data to calculate output pixel results. As the four-pixel blocks are read from the three lines, they are accumulated in half of the pixel data buffer, capable of storing 12 pixels. These data are used by the group processor to calculate the associated output pixel values. When new pixel data are needed, the next three blocks are read and placed in the other half of the buffer. Again, output pixels are calculated. When the next batch of pixel data is needed, the image store is read and the pixel data are placed in the first half of the buffer where the previously loaded pixels have already been used and are no longer needed. This ping-pong effect in the pixel data buffer minimizes buffer size by over-writing spent input pixel data with new data.

The coefficient buffer is a nine location buffer by eight bits wide. Its purpose is to store the nine coefficients of the convolution kernel for the required group operation. The coefficients are represented by a 7-bit binary number of the form XXXX.XXX and a sign bit. The overall decimal range is therefore, − 15.875 to + 15.875, with a resolution of 0.125. As seen in the various kernels overviewed in Chapter 5, this range is basically adequate for the coefficients needed. Coefficients are loaded into the coefficient buffer by the host computer and are then sequenced out by the group processor as needed.

The heart of the group processor is the calculation circuitry, illustrated in Figure 7-8. This hardware takes sequenced pixel and coefficient data and produces output pixel values. The processor is composed of a multiplier, adder/subtractor, accumulator, and four output pixel latches. The basic operation takes pixel and coefficient data, multiplies the two, accumulates nine such sequences, and stores the result in one of four output latches. Once four output pixels have been calculated and loaded into the output latches, a write is done to the output image store.

Figure 7-8 Pixel group processor calculation hardware.

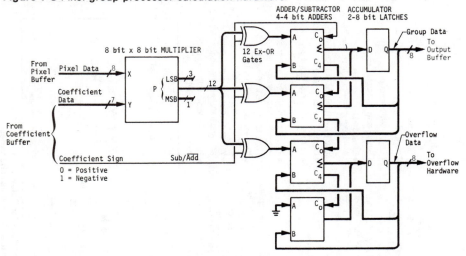

The multiplier to be used in the calculation circuitry is a high-speed bipolar type. One such chip is the TRW, LSI Products Division MPY-8HUJ, capable of multiplying two 8-bit integers in less than 100nS (see Figure 7-9). The chip generates a product that is a binary number of 16 bits. In the case of the group processor, we will be multiplying an 8-bit pixel by a 7-bit coefficient which means that the

LSI Multipliers, HJ Series

Models:
MPY-8HJ (8x8 bit)
MPY-8HJ-1 (8x8 bit)
MPY-8HUJ (8x8 bit)
MPY-8HUJ-1 (8x8 bit)
MPY-12HJ (12x12 bit)
MPY-16HJ (16x16 bit)

The HJ devices have better than a 2-to-1 speed-power improvement over the MPY AJ series multipliers.

Features
- n-by-n parallel array multiplier, n = 8, 12, or 16
- Double precision product
- 45 to 100 nsec typical multiply time
- Much lower power/less space than MSI equivalent multipliers
- Includes input/output registers
- Single chip, bipolar TTL technology
- Single bus or multiport operation
- Radiation hard
- Three-state outputs
- Single power supply, +5V
- Extended temperature range available for military applications

New Features of HJ Series
- Higher speed/lower power
- Zero-nanosecond register hold time (Typically)
- Two's complement, unsigned magnitude, or mixed-mode (12 x 12 and 16 x 16 only)
- Easily expandable for larger array multiplication
- Worst case specs across full voltage and temperature ranges
- Pin-compatible with AJ series multipliers (except MPY-8HUJ)

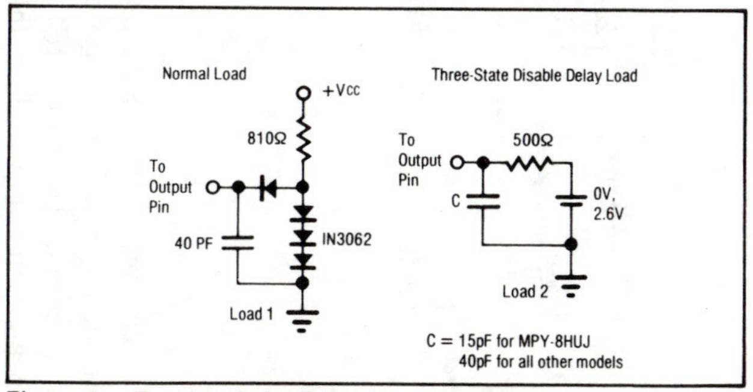

The MPY LSI multipliers are high speed, TTL LSI devices. They are n-by-n parallel array multipliers with double precision outputs. Their low power and high performance characteristics are the result of a proven method developed and patented by TRW (U.S. Patent No. 3,900,724). Fundamental TTL devices used to produce the MPY-LSI were also developed and patented by TRW (U.S. Patent No. 3,283,170). The major multiplier array logic achieves speed-power performance of less than 1 picojoule per equivalent gate.

Four input/output registers are used in the MPY LSI multipliers. These registers are D-type flip-flops with a single phase positive edge triggered TTL clock.

Applications for MPY LSI multipliers include digital processing and high speed multiplication for fast Fourier transforms. They are ideal for extending the capabilities of mini/microcomputers, permitting hardware multiplication for increased computational speed.

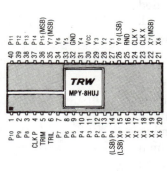

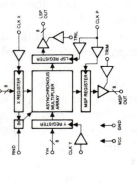

Logic Block Diagram

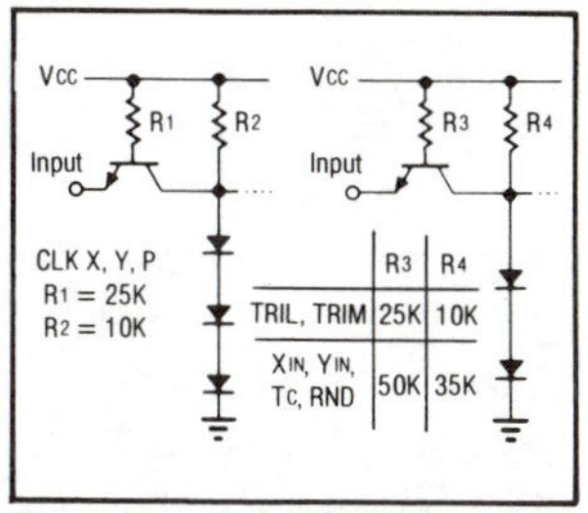

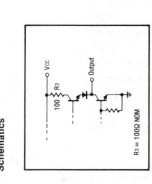

Figure 2 — Equivalent Input Schematics

R3 = 100Ω NOM

Figure 3 — Output Schematic

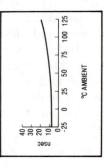

Figure 4 — Typical Setup Time

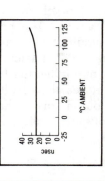

Figure 5 — Typical Three-State Disable Delay, Output Delay

Three-State Disable Delay Load

C = 15pF for MPY-8HUJ
40pF for all other models

Normal Load

**Figure 1 — Test Loads for Delay Measurements
Figures 1-5 Apply to all Multipliers in HJ Series**

Figure 7-9 Typical 8-bit × 8-bit bipolar multiplier. (Reprinted by permission of TRW Inc., LSI Products Division, copyright © 1981.)

largest product in our calculations will be of 15 bits. How-ever, since the coefficient includes three fractional bits, the least significant three bits are thrown out after the multi-ply, leaving 12 bits of integer product. The calculation of a single output pixel requires the accumulation of nine such products; therefore, we follow the output of the multiplier with an adder/subtracter, composed of the exclusive OR gates and 74S283 adders. The adder/subtracter must be ca-pable of addition and subtraction as dictated by the coeffi-cient sign bit which is fed around the multiply circuitry to the adder/subtracter. Subsequently, the result of the adder/subtracter is passed to an accumulator made up of 8-bit latches. Figure 7-10 illustrates the 74S283 binary ad-der.

TTL
MSI

**TYPES SN54283, SN54LS283, SN54S283,
SN74283, SN74LS283, SN74S283
4-BIT BINARY FULL ADDERS WITH FAST CARRY**
BULLETIN NO. DL-S 7611832, OCTOBER 1976

- Full-Carry Look-Ahead Across the Four Bits
- Systems Achieve Partial Look-Ahead Performance with the Economy of Ripple Carry
- Supply Voltage and Ground on Corner Pins to Simplify P-C Board Layout

TYPICAL ADD TIMES

TYPE	TWO 8-BIT WORDS	TWO 16-BIT WORDS	TYPICAL POWER DISSIPATION PER ADDER
'283	23ns	43ns	310 mW
'LS283	25ns	45ns	95 mW
'S283	15ns	30ns	510 mW

SN54283, SN54LS283 . . . J OR W PACKAGE
SN54S283 . . . J PACKAGE
SN74283, SN74LS283, SN74S283 . . . J OR N PACKAGE
(TOP VIEW)

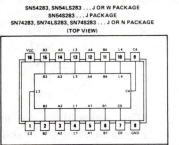

positive logic: see function table

description

The '283 and 'LS283 adders are electrically and functionally identical to the '83A and 'LS283, respectively; only the arrangement of the terminals has been changed. The 'S283 high performance versions are also functionally identical.

These improved full adders perform the addition of two 4-bit binary words. The sum (Σ) outputs are provided for each bit and the resultant carry (C4) is obtained from the fourth bit. These adders feature full internal look-ahead across all four bits generating the carry term in ten nanoseconds, typically, for the '283 and 'LS283, and 7.5 nanoseconds for the 'S283. This capability provides the system designer with partial look-ahead performance at the economy and reduced package count of a ripple-carry implementation.

The adder logic, including the carry, is implemented in its true form. End around carry can be accomplish-ed without the need for logic or level inversion.

Series 54, Series 54LS, and Series 54S circuits are characterized for operation over the full temperature range of $-55°C$ to $125°C$. Series 74, Series 74LS, and Series 74S circuits are characterized for $0°C$ to $70°C$ operation.

FUNCTION TABLE

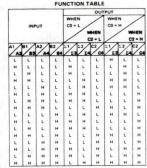

INPUT				OUTPUT					
				WHEN C0 = L			WHEN C0 = H		
					WHEN C2 = L			WHEN C2 = H	
A1 A3	B1 B3	A2 A4	B2 B4	Σ1 Σ3	Σ2 Σ4	C2 C4	Σ1 Σ3	Σ2 Σ4	C2 C4
L	L	L	L	L	L	L	H	L	L
H	L	L	L	H	L	L	L	H	L
L	H	L	L	H	L	L	L	H	L
H	H	L	L	L	H	L	H	H	L
L	L	H	L	L	H	L	H	H	L
H	L	H	L	H	H	L	L	L	H
L	H	H	L	H	H	L	L	L	H
H	H	H	L	L	L	H	H	L	H
L	L	L	H	L	H	L	H	H	L
H	L	L	H	H	H	L	L	L	H
L	H	L	H	H	H	L	L	L	H
H	H	L	H	L	L	H	H	L	H
L	L	H	H	L	L	H	H	L	H
H	L	H	H	H	L	H	L	H	H
L	H	H	H	H	L	H	L	H	H
H	H	H	H	L	H	H	H	H	H

H = high level, L = low level
NOTE: Input conditions at A1, B1, A2, B2, and C0 are used to determine outputs Σ1 and Σ2 and the value of the internal carry C2. The values at C2, A3, B3, A4, and B4 are then used to determine outputs Σ3, Σ4, and C4.

TEXAS INSTRUMENTS
INCORPORATED
POST OFFICE BOX 5012 • DALLAS, TEXAS 75222

Figure 7-10 74S283 4-bit binary adder. (Reprinted by permission of Texas Instruments Incorporation, copyright © 1981.)

The method employed by the adder/subtracter is two's complement arithmetic allowing the handling of positive and negative numbers. As a refresher, the convention of the two's complement numbering scheme as applied to a 4-bit number is listed:

Decimal	Binary 2's Complement
7	0111
6	0110
5	0101
4	0100
3	0011
2	0010
1	0001
0	0000
−1	1111
−2	1110
−3	1101
−4	1100
−5	1011
−6	1010
−7	1001
−8	1000

The major thing to remember is that to carry out a two's complement subtraction, the positive number being subtracted is inverted and 1 is added, yielding a two's complement negative number. This number is then added to the accumulator, effecting the subtraction. For this reason, exclusive OR gates are between the multiplier and adders to allow inversion of the data. When one input to an XOR gate is low, the output follows the other input. However, when one input is high, the output will be the inverse of the other input. With the coefficient sign bit acting as one input to the XOR gates, the data may be inverted or not as required by the original sign of the coefficient. In addition to inverting the data, the two's complement convention requires that a 1 must be added to the number. This may be done by setting the carry input of the adder to the active, or high state. Again, this is done by the coefficient sign bit. When a subtract is done, the XOR gates invert the data and the adder carry input is set high so that the add now is actually adding a negative number—equivalent to subtracting a positive number.

For a normal cycle of nine multiplications and nine additions/subtractions, first the accumulator latches are cleared. The first pixel and coefficient are then both addressed and enabled to flow from their respective buffers to the multiplier. The coefficient sign bit goes directly to the XOR gates and carry input of the adder. At some point, data are assumed stable at the multiplier inputs, and the multiplier input clocks are strobed. 100nS later the multiply is complete and its output clock is strobed, allowing the product to flow to the XOR gates. Depending on the coefficient sign bit, the data will either be inverted or not and will proceed to the adders. Some time later, the correct result is present at the adder outputs and the accumulator latch inputs. The accumulator is strobed, storing the first result.

The accumulator outputs are fed back to the second operand inputs of the adders so that during the upcoming cycle, the new product will be added or subtracted to the current partial result residing in the accumulator. The same cycle occurs nine times and, ultimately yields the output pixel result at the outputs of the accumulator. This result is then strobed into the proper output latch. When all four output latches are full, the four output pixels are written to the output image store.

Each multiply/accumulate cycle can be done in 200nS. This time is derived from the 100nS multiply time added to the sum of the propagation times found in the XOR gates and adders along with the accumulator setup time. Given the 200nS cycle time and the requirement of nine cycles per output pixel, we find that the time to generate a new output pixel requires $9 \times 200nS = 1.80\mu S$. Since all image store accesses are four pixels wide, we require $4 \times 1.80\mu S = 7.20\mu S$ plus three reads and a write access time, $4 \times 616.1nS = 2.464\mu S$, to completely process four pixels. An entire image frame of 256×256, then, has a total processing time of 64 blocks of 4 pixels $\times$ (7.2μS calculation time $+$ 2.464μS access time) $\times$ 256 lines $= 158.4mS$. This amounts to just under five frame times; very respectable, given the simplicity and low cost of this group processor hardware.

As we recall from Chapter 5, the sum of the coefficients in a defined convolution kernel is always 0 or 1. Given the case of the coefficients adding to one and all pixels in the calculation having the full value of 255, the output calculation will never exceed eight bits. The data out of the accumulator reside in the low-order eight bits of the 16-bit field and, at the end of nine cycles, will become the output pixel value. The 16 bits must be present during the calculation because the partial result may overflow the low-order eight bits at any time, depending on the coefficients and their orientation within the convolution kernel being used. So, the low-order eight bits feed from the accumulator latches to the output latches. The high-order bits should always be zero. Overflow circuitry may watch these bits and indicate an overflow condition if they do not equal zero at the end of an output pixel calculation (see Figure 7-11). The only time that an overflow condition should occur is when the coefficients do not add to 1 or less than 1.

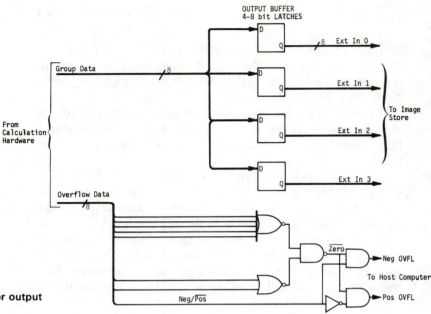

Figure 7-11 Pixel group processor output buffers and overflow hardware.

SCHOTTKY†
TTL MEMORIES

TYPES SN54S189A, SN54S289A, SN74S189A, SN74S289A
64-BIT HIGH-PERFORMANCE
RANDOM-ACCESS MEMORIES

SEPTEMBER 1976—REVISED JUNE 1979

STATIC RANDOM-ACCESS MEMORIES

- Fully Decoded RAM's Organized as 16 Words of Four Bits Each
- Schottky-Clamped for High Speed:
  Read Cycle Time . . . 25 ns Typical
  Write Cycle Time . . . 25 ns Typical
- Choice of Three-State or Open-Collector Outputs
- Compatible with Most TTL and I²L Circuits
- Chip-Select Input Simplifies External Decoding

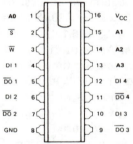

SN54S189A, SN54S289A . . . . J OR W PACKAGE
SN74S189A, SN74S289A . . . . J OR N PACKAGE
(TOP VIEW)

A0	1	16	V_CC
S̄	2	15	A1
W̄	3	14	A2
DI 1	4	13	A3
D̄O̅ 1	5	12	DI 4
DI 2	6	11	D̄O̅ 4
D̄O̅ 2	7	10	DI 3
GND	8	9	D̄O̅ 3

Pin assignments are same for all packages.

description

These 64-bit active-element memories are monolithic Schottky-clamped transistor-transistor logic (TTL) arrays organized as 16 words of four bits each. They are fully decoded and feature a chip-select input to simplify decoding required to achieve expanded system organization. The memories feature p-n-p input transistors that reduce the low-level input current requirement to a maximum of −0.25 milliamperes, only one-eighth that of a Series 54S/74S standard load factor. The chip-select circuitry is implemented with minimal delay times to compensate for added system decoding.

write cycle

The information applied at the data input is written into the selected location when the chip-select input and the write-enable input are low. While the write-enable input is low, the 'S189A output is in the high-impedance state and the 'S289A output is off. When a number of outputs are bus-connected, this high-impedance or off state will neither load nor drive the bus line, but it will allow the bus line to be driven by another active output or a passive pull-up.

read cycle

The stored information (complement of information applied at the data input during the write cycle) is available at the output when the write-enable input is high and the chip-select input is low. When the chip-select input is high, the 'S189A output will be in the high-impedance state and the 'S289A output will be off.

FUNCTION TABLE

FUNCTION	INPUTS		'S189A OUTPUT	'S289A OUTPUT
	CHIP SELECT	WRITE ENABLE		
Write	L	L	High Impedance	Off
Read	L	H	Complement of Data Entered	Complement of Data Entered
Inhibit	H	X	High Impedance	Off

H – high level, L – low level, X – irrelevant

Figure 7-12 74S189 16 × 4-bit scratch pad Static RAM. (Reprinted by permission of Texas Instruments Incorporated, copyright © 1979.)

TEXAS INSTRUMENTS
INCORPORATED
POST OFFICE BOX 225012 • DALLAS, TEXAS 75265

An item that was glossed over earlier is that of pixel and coefficient buffer sequencing. The coefficient buffer sequencing is not complicated. Before initiating a group process, the host computer must load the nine kernel coefficients into the coefficient buffer. This buffer is composed of high-speed scratch pad static RAM memory. A suitable chip is the 74S189, a 16 × 4 bit RAM. The 74S189 specification sheet is shown in Figure 7-12. The nine coefficients may be loaded in any order as long as they are sequenced out in the same 3 × 3 spatial order as the pixels from the pixel buffer. We will adopt the convention of sequentially loading the coefficients in the order A through I as defined in Chapter 5. During the nine cycles of the group processor, the coefficients will be sequenced out in the same order. Remember, the coefficients remain constant throughout the entire image operation. The coefficient buffer is illustrated in Figure 7-13.

Figure 7-13 Pixel group processor coefficient buffer.

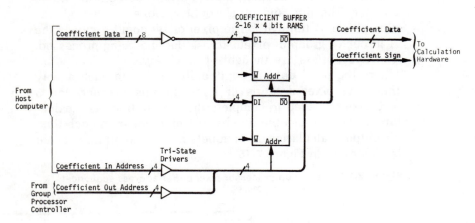

Pixel buffer loading and sequencing becomes a bit more difficult. As we recall from the previous chapter, it is necessary to load three line groups of four pixels each. The pixel buffer is broken into two sections, we will call them pixel buffer 0 and 1. Each buffer is capable of storing 12 pixels—three lines of four pixels each. Once the pixel data from one buffer is nearly spent, the other is loaded with the next 12 pixels. This ping-pong effect occurs every time new pixel data is needed. Figure 7-14 illustrates the pixel buffer scheme. Loading will occur whenever the detection is made that data from either buffer are fully used, or are no longer useful in the calculation of subsequent output pixels in the line being processed.

123

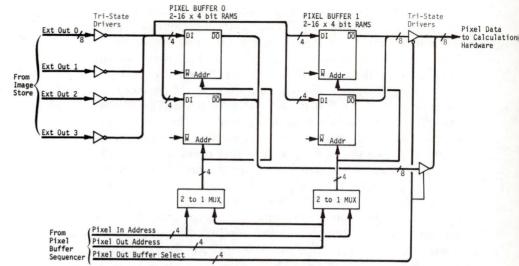

Figure 7-14 Pixel group processor pixel buffer.

In the sequencing-out of pixel data, the addressing may be thought of as being made up of three address counters—a pixel counter, a pixel offset counter, and a line counter. The line and pixel counter sequence through the nine pixels, A through I. The pixel offset counter moves the A through I group of pixels across the line being processed. The two buffers are thought of as a single circular buffer, where the pixel data is continually loaded in such a way that new pixel data never ends. In this manner, the 3 × 3 pixels needed to complete the next output pixel calculation creep across the line by one pixel location each time an output calculation is completed. This counting scheme is illustrated in Figure 7-15.

Figure 7-15 Pixel group processor pixel buffer address sequencer.

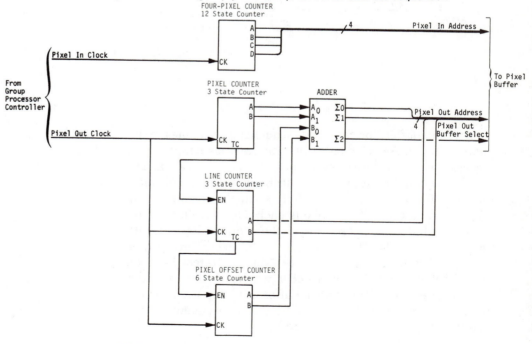

By properly controlling the loading and output sequencing of the pixel data in unison with the constant coefficient data, the group processor arithmetic circuitry stays in continuous operation.

We have now defined a complete group processor capable of speedy, yet low-cost implementation. The processing of a 256 × 256 image frame in five frame times yields more-than-adequate processing power for most general applications.

Frame Processor

Frame processing, as described in Chapter 5, breaks down to rather special-purpose processes having little in common with one another. Because of this, hardware to carry out such processes is usually considered nonstandard. In contrast, point and group processes do well to have their own dedicated hardware because they cover a wide range of image operations, all commonly used in most image processing applications. For an image processor designed for a particular special-purpose application, the addition of various frame processing circuits in hardware can be advantageous in a processing-time sense. A general-purpose image processing system, however, rarely warrants the cost involved in supplying this type of hardware.

For this reason, we will not discuss actual hardware implementations of frame processes. Instead, these processes will remain reserved for software processing through the host computer. In frame processing, the low-end image processing system simply becomes the means in which to capture, store, and display images allowing image data access, reads, and writes by the host computer.

As seen in previous chapters, an external access cycle is available to transfer image data in and out of the image store. In the previous image processing hardware discussions, the external access cycle was used to get data between the image store and the processing hardware. For frame processing, though, the path will be between the image store and the host computer. As always, pixels are transferred in chunks of four per access.

Recalling geometric operations discussed in Chapter 5, all processing takes input pixel data and maps it into new spatial locations. In the case of scaling and rotation, an interpolation algorithm was employed when the pixel mapping was not one to one. These operations may be handled by the host computer reading input pixel data from an input image store, processing the data through the geometric routines, and writing the result (or partial result) into an output image store. The time of processing becomes a function of the computational speed of the host computer.

It is possible, however, to calculate the time needed to access image data in and out of the image stores. In a normal cycle, the host will read four pixels, process them, write the results to the output store, and read the next four pixels. The total time needed for a 256 × 256 image, then, requires two external access cycle times per four pixels leading to the overall image data input/output time of 2 × 616.1nS external access cycle time × 64 pixel blocks of 4 × 256 lines = 20.19mS. The overall frame processing time will be this input/output time, added to the product of the host computer processing time per pixel and the number of pixels in the frame.

Image transforms require the same image data input/output time as did the geometric operations, 20.19mS. These operations are generally very time consuming, no matter how they are implemented. For applications requiring lots of image transform operations, it is often a stringent requirement that some sort of hardware processing be available. One common method of meeting reasonable processing times is to attach an array processor to the host system. Array processors are special-purpose number-crunching hardware systems specially designed for the rapid arithmetic processing of numbers. In this scheme, the host computer controls the accessing of image data from the image processing system and carries out the required operations with the help of the array processor.

In data compression processing, image data are read into the host computer from the input image store but never written back to an output store. As we recall, the purpose of data compression is for data bit reduction in data transmission and bulk memory storage. Therefore, the host will write the results to another device, such as a telemetry system or bulk memory peripheral. The input time needed will be 616.1nS external access cycle time × 64 pixel blocks of 4 × 256 lines = 10.09mS for a 256 × 256 image. The total processing time will, again, be a function of the speed of the host processor.

For low-cost image processing, the frame processes are regarded as special purpose, not to be handled by the on-board image processing hardware. The use of software processing by the host computer is often satisfactory because of the lower frequency of need of these processes by the user. The upgrade to a system with good overall frame processing time characteristics requires the proper selection of a suitable host computer, as well as, in some cases, the addition of an array processor peripheral.

PROCESSING IN ACTION IV

We have encountered a wide variety of digital image processing operations in the preceding chapters of this book. To facilitate the structure of presentation, however, these operations were discussed in the context of their implementation processes. Because of this, easy reference to a given operation is somewhat hindered.

In Part IV the commonly used digital image processing operations have been consolidated by presenting them in a catalog form. This section represents application groups—contrast enhancement, spatial filtering, edge enhancement, geometric manipulations, and other operations.

Each Image Operation Study contains a concise rundown of the functions, implementations, and drawbacks, as well as several before-and-after photographs of a selected operation. Part IV provides quick, concise explanations of these operations without the instructional overhead seen earlier.

Image Operation Studies

Image Operation Study # 1

Operation—Binary Contrast Enhancement

Description—Binary contrast enhancement is an operation used to process an input image into a high-contrast output image consisting of two gray levels, black and white. Pixel gray levels in the input image are individually compared to a selected threshold value. For an input pixel level less than the threshold value, the corresponding output pixel is set to black. Otherwise, the output pixel is set to white. The resulting image is, therefore, composed of black and white pixels, based on the brightness comparisons of the input pixel gray levels and the threshold value.

Application—This enhancement is particularly useful in the extraction of object boundaries from their background when the gray levels between the two are very close. For instance, printed text that has faded or is viewed under low-light-level conditions may be barely discernable from the surface in which it is printed. As long as there exists at least one gray-level difference between the text and its background surface, however, this enhancement will separate the two. A threshold gray level is selected so that the gray level of the text is less and the background more. The result is an output image with the text appearing black and the background white.

Another use for this enhancement is in manufacturing process control applications. Take, for instance, the requirement of automatically measuring the area of a hole in a piece of aluminum. This procedure may be carried out repetitively on specimens traveling down a conveyor under a television camera feeding a simple image processor. The measurement is done by counting the number of pixels that make up the hole. In order to do this, a binary contrast enhancement is performed first. The selection of an appropriate threshold value yields a processed image where the hole appears as black pixels and the rest as white. The hole area may then be calculated by counting all black pixels appearing in the image. This count is readily available from the output image histogram.

Cautions — A difficulty arises with the binary contrast enhancement when the object and its background have common or overlapping gray levels. In this case, it is not possible to choose a threshold value so that all object pixels will go to one level and all background pixels to the other. The resulting output image will not display a good separation between object and background.

Implementation—Single image/pixel point operation. The map will always be a step function, with the transition occurring at the chosen threshold level.

Results

Figure IOS1-1
(a) Original low light level image.

(b) Binary contrast map used to separate book title words from background.

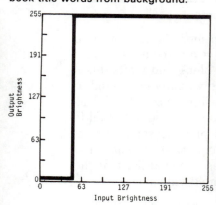

(c) Output image with words"Digital Image Processing" clearly visible.

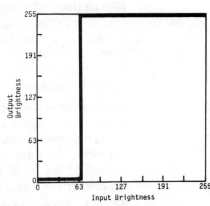

Figure IOS1-2
(a) Original image of machined part.

(b) Binary contrast map used to highlight machined hole diameter.

(c) Output image.

Image Operation Study #2

Operation—Histogram Sliding

Description—Histogram sliding is an enhancement used to add or subtract a constant brightness to all pixels within an image. In the context of a histogram, the effect of this operation is to yield an output image with a histogram that is shifted either to the right or left from that of the input image histogram.

Application—This operation has the visible effect of brightening or darkening an image scene. Since the histogram of the processed image is only shifted and otherwise remains the same, the contrast of the output image will be identical to that of the input image. For use in general contrast enhancement operations, this process may be used to slide the gray level range into a new range facilitating subsequent operations.

Cautions—When doing a histogram slide, be careful of gray level saturation. This occurs when such a constant is added or subtracted that pixels in the input image overflow at the black or white level. For instance, when a value is added to the pixels of an input image the effect is to slide the image histogram to the right. If, however, the slide is too great, pixels will bunch up at the white level. This is because their constant value added to the original gray level totaled to more than the maximum white level. When this happens brightness resolution is lost. Before doing a slide, it is a good idea to preview the input image histogram, taking note of the minimum and maximum gray levels present in the image. To preclude saturation effects, a slide constant must be chosen that will not push the maximum gray level past the full white level or the minimum level past the full black level.

Implementation — Single image/pixel point operation The map will always be a 45° line. In the case of a slide of zero, the line will pass through the origin.

Results

Figure IOS2-1
(a) Original image.

(b) Original image histogram.

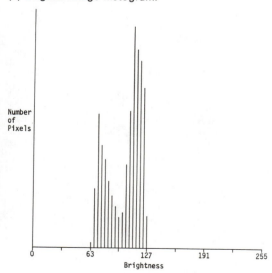

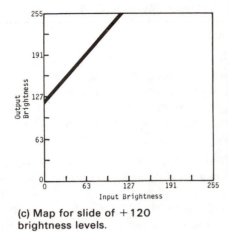

(c) Map for slide of +120 brightness levels.

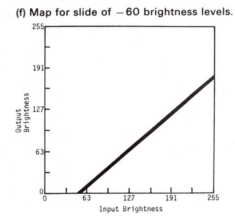

(d) Result of +120 slide.

(e) Histogram after +120 slide.

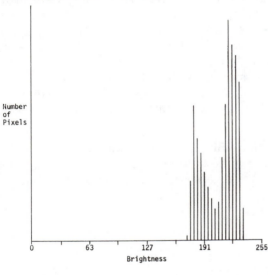

(f) Map for slide of −60 brightness levels.

(h) Histogram after −60 slide.

(g) Result of −60 slide.

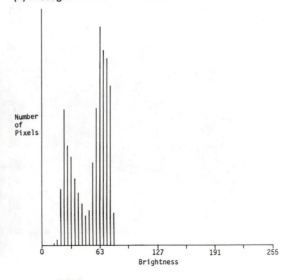

133

Image Operation Study #3

Operation—Histogram Stretching

Description—Histogram stretching is a contrast enhancement that allows multiplication and division of all pixel brightnesses within an image by a constant value. This has the effect of stretching or shrinking the input image histogram, thereby controlling the gray level range of the output image histogram.

Application—The apparent effect of this process upon an image is to increase or decrease its contrast. The stretching operation expands or reduces the contrast and dynamic range of the image. General contrast enhancements may be carried out with this operation in conjunction with others such as histogram sliding.

Cautions—Because of the multiplication of pixel brightnesses by constants, it is very easy to overflow the allowed white level in a given gray scale. Care in the selection of multiplicative constants must be exercised so that overflow saturation is prevented. Additionally, an important artifact of the division of pixel brightnesses by a contrast is brightness resolution loss. For instance, dividing pixel brightnesses in an input image by two shrinks the histogram of the image by a factor of two, making it readily apparent that gray scale occupancy has also been halved.

Implementation—Single image/pixel point process This map will always be a straight line passing through the origin. In the case of a stretch by a factor of 1, the line will be 45°.

Results

Figure IOS3-1
(a) Original image.

(b) Original image histogram.

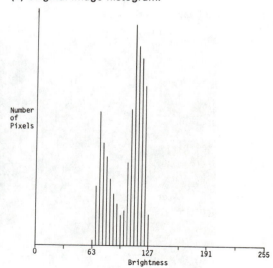

134

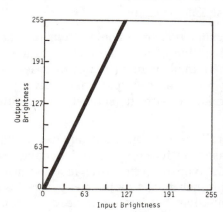

(c) Map for brightness stretch of 2.

(d) Result of times 2 stretch.

(e) Histogram after times 2 stretch.

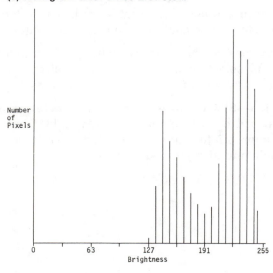

(f) Map for brightness shrink by factor of 2.

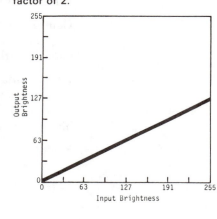

(h) Histogram after shrink by 2.

(g) Result of shrink by 2.

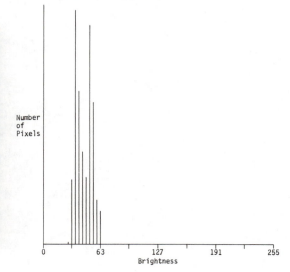

135

Image Operation Study #4

Operation—Contrast Enhancement

Description—The common case of contrast enhancement is made up of a combination of both the histogram slide and stretch operations. By implementing both processes in one operation, we may produce an output image having a histogram dictating an image with the subjective attributes of good contrast.

Application—General contrast enhancement serves to improve an image based on its contrast and dynamic range characteristics. This type of processing is often used to correct an image for such things as poor exposure and improper scene illumination. An important need for contrast enhancement is in the clean-up of an image preceding or following other processing. Often the results of other operations will leave artifacts based on the algorithms employed. These artifacts, when undesired, may often be corrected for using basic contrast enhancement techniques.

Cautions—As seen in the histogram slide and stretch examples, careful selection of constants is required to preclude overflow and gross resolution loss conditions.

Implementation—Single image/pixel point operation The map is composed by the combination of two LUTs as derived from appropriate slide and stretch operations; see histogram slide and histogram stretch examples.

Results

Figure IOS4-1
(a) Original image.

(b) Original image histogram.

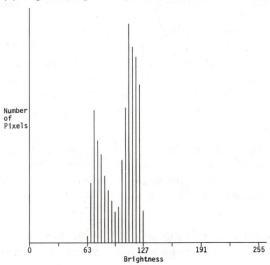

(c) Map for slide of −60 and stretch of 4.

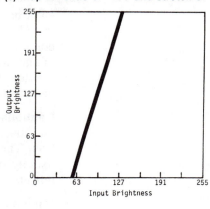

(e) Histogram after slide and stretch.

(d) Result of slide and stretch.

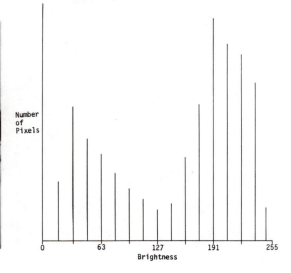

137

Image Operation Study # 5

Operation—Complement Image

Description—A complement image is an image where all pixel brightnesses are logically complemented, or reversed. Black pixels become white, white pixels become black, and the gray levels in between take on their respective reverse brightnesses. The end result is a negative image having the same appearance as a film negative of the original.

Application—This process is often useful in the analysis of an image. Because the eye responds logarithmically to brightness changes, details characterized by small brightness deviations in the white regions may be undetectable. Complementing the image converts these small changes in the white regions to the black regions, where they are more visible. Although the image takes on a rather unnatural appearance, analysis of fine details hidden in bright regions is often aided.

Partial complementing of an image also produces results helpful to the analyst. An example would be to leave the lower half of the gray scale untouched while complementing the upper half. Dark regions in the original image are unaffected while bright regions are complemented down into the dark regions where details are often more visible.

Cautions—The process of partial image complementing may be tailored to give the best results for a given application. The area of the gray scale to be complemented may usually be chosen by trial techniques. The final selection is left up to visual comparison.

Implementation—Single image/pixel point process The portion of the gray scale to be complemented uses a map appearing as a 45° line traversing downward, left to right.

Results

Figure IOS5-1
(a) Original image of flowers.

(c) Result of full complement.

(b) Map for full brightness complement.

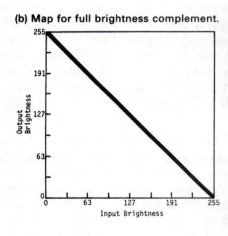

(d) Map for complement of bright regions only.

(e) Result of bright region complement.

Image Operation Study # 6

Operation—Low Pass Filter

Description—Low pass filtering of an image produces an output image in which high spatial frequency components have been attenuated. The cutoff point at which higher frequencies become attenuated is varied by the selection of mask weighting coefficients.

Application—Low pass filtering is employed as a smoothing operation to reduce high spatial frequency components that may be present in an image. In particular, this operation is useful in removing visual noise, which generally appears as sharp bright points. Because of the very high spatial frequency in these "spikes," the low pass filter acts well in their attenuation.

Low pass filters also are used to simply reduce high-frequency components in order to more closely examine the low-frequency content of an image. For instance, say the object of interest in an image is a cloud formation and a distracting telephone cable appears silhouetted in front. We may use a low pass filter to attenuate the cable while leaving the cloud relatively untouched. This is because the cloud is basically composed of low-frequency components and the cable contains high-frequency components. This filtering operation will attenuate the cable with little effect to the cloud.

Cautions—Because of the limitations of a 3×3 kernel size in carrying out group processes, the spatial frequency at which the low pass filter begins attenuation is not highly selectable. As a result, the output image will often be either over- or under-filtered for a given application. For this reason, it is easy to lose high-frequency information that was intended to be retained. The optimum mask to be used is a tradeoff issue, usually determined by visual inspection of the results.

Implementation—Group process The mask coefficients will always add to 1. All coefficients are positive and, therefore, fractional. Three typical masks are given:

1/9	1/9	1/9		1/10	1/10	1/10		1/16	1/8	1/16
1/9	1/9	1/9		1/10	1/5	1/10		1/8	1/4	1/8
1/9	1/9	1/9		1/10	1/10	1/10		1/16	1/8	1/16

| Mask 1 | Mask 2 | Mask 3 |

Results

Figure IOS6-1
(a) Original image.

(b) Result of low pass mask #1.

(c) Result of low pass mask #2.

(d) Result of low pass mask #3.

Image Operation Study #7

Operation—High Pass Filter

Description—High pass filtering of an image produces an output image in which high spatial frequency components are accentuated. The cutoff point at which higher frequencies become accentuated is varied by the selection of mask weighting coefficients.

Application—High pass filtering is used in the enhancement of edges and other high-frequency components within an image. Images that do not appear clear may be sharpened by high pass filtering. The sharpness of an image is related to the content of high spatial frequency components within the image. Therefore, the high pass filter serves well in the enhancement.

Additionally, this filter is useful any time it is desired to enhance high spatial frequencies for viewability of certain features. An example of this might be the enhancement of a spatially detailed object—say, a tree appearing in front of flat surface such as dirt-covered ground. The effect of the filter will be to enhance the tree while leaving the ground relatively untouched.

Cautions—As in the case of the low pass filter, cutoff frequency is not highly selectable when using the standard 3 × 3 kernel size. The final mask selection most appropriate to a given application is generally determined by comparative visual inspection.

Implementation—Group process The mask coefficients always add to 1. A large coefficient will generally appear in the center of the mask surrounded by smaller positive and negative coefficients. Three typical masks are given.

$$\begin{array}{ccc} -1 & -1 & -1 \\ -1 & 9 & -1 \\ -1 & -1 & -1 \end{array} \qquad \begin{array}{ccc} 0 & -1 & 0 \\ -1 & 5 & -1 \\ 0 & -1 & 0 \end{array} \qquad \begin{array}{ccc} 1 & -2 & 1 \\ -2 & 5 & -2 \\ 1 & -2 & 1 \end{array}$$

Mask 1   Mask 2   Mask 3

Results

Figure IOS7-1
(a) Original image.

(b) Result of high pass mask #1.

(c) Result of high pass mask #2.

(d) Result of high pass mask #3.

Image Operation Study # 8

Operation—Median Filter

Description—The median filter is a group-like process operating on a 3 × 3 pixel neighborhood. It does not fall within the category of a spatial convolution, however, because its result is not based on a weighted average of the nine pixels in the neighborhood. Instead, the output of the median filter is the median value of the nine pixel brightness values. The median value of a neighborhood is determined by placing the nine brightnesses into ascending numerical order and selecting the center value such that four values are less than or equal to and four greater than or equal to the center value. This center value becomes the output pixel in the calculation.

Application—The primary use for the median filter is in pictorial noise removal. Noise spikes appear as bright pixels randomly distributed across an image. Since these spikes are bright in comparison with their neighbors, they generally end up near the top when the nine pixels are placed in ascending order. The median value tends to reduce any influence from the spike itself.

An interesting use for this filter is in art applications. When applied several times, an image begins to look as if it were hand painted. Details tend to look brushed on. Using the median filter, real-life images may be processed into synthetic paintings. Adding the effects of other operations may generate additional interesting effects.

Cautions—The median filter is somewhat unpredictable, often leaving an image worse off than it was initially. The greatest loss is suffered in details composed of high spatial frequencies. These regions become somewhat distorted. The tradeoff is worth it, though, if an image is badly speckled with white noise spikes, because the resulting output image will be virtually spike-free.

Implementation—Group process (frame process) The median filter operates similar to a group process, deriving its results from 3 × 3 neighborhoods of pixels. However, it is not a convolution operation and is therefore not handled by hardware used in general group processing. For this reason, the median filter is most often implemented in software through a host computer. Since the group process hardware is not used, it is probably more suitable to call the operation a frame process. Spike suppression is illustrated on a typical 3 × 3 neighborhood. All of the brightnesses in the group are between 5 and 20 except for the center pixel, which is 210. This "white spike" is ultimately replaced with the value of 15, eliminating its distracting effect on the image.

Pixel brightness
in a 3×3 group   Brightness values placed in ascending order

```
10    20    5
15    210   20      5 10 10 15 15 20 20 20 210
15    10    20                  ↑
                     Median value = Result to replace
                                    group center pixel
```

Results

Figure IOS8-1

(a) Original image with noise spikes.

(b) Result after median filtered.

(d) Result after application of the median filter twice — the painted appearance is evident.

(c) Original image.

Image Operation Study #9

Operation—Unsharp Masking Enhancement

Description—The unsharp masking enhancement produces an output image in which high-frequency details are improved. Lower-frequency regions of the image are left basically untouched. This process generally yields a more subtle and visually appealing enhancement than that of the high pass filter. It is interesting to note that this operation is borrowed from the photographic darkroom, where it is commonly used.

The enhancement is formed by the subtraction of a low pass filtered image from its original. The idea being that edges in the low passed image are changing more slowly than their counterparts in the original. When a slower-changing transition is subtracted from a faster one, the result is a transition with overshoot and undershoot. This translates to edge accentuation. This phenomenon is illustrated:

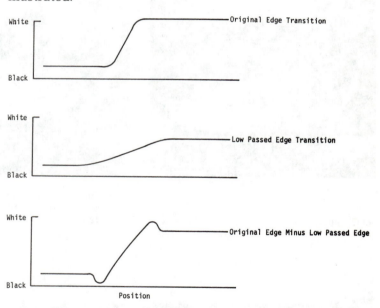

Figure IOS9-1
Unsharp masking edge accentuation.

Prior to subtraction, the low passed image may be brightness scaled by a histogram shrink (stretch) operation. This has the effect of controlling the amount of accentuation to occur in the enhancement.

Application—The unsharp masking operation produces an output image that appears sharpened, remaining visually appealing. Because of this, it is often employed to simply sharpen images suffering from some sort of blurring. Examples of blurred cases may include images exhibiting very poor contrast, haze obstruction, or even minor defocus.

Cautions—The variables in this process are (1) the extent of low pass filtering to be evoked upon the original image before subtraction and (2) the amount of brightness scaling to be used on the low passed image before subtracting it from the original. The amount of low pass filtering affects the amount of the over- and undershoot components in the final image transitions. Brightness scaling has an impact on how accentuated the edges will appear and how attenuated the low-frequency regions will be. For instance, large brightness scaling will leave the original minimally changed in low-frequency areas but also will not accentuate the edges to a high degree. On the other hand, no scaling allows the low-frequency regions to be almost entirely subtracted out to black while the edges will be highly accentuated. A good tradeoff brightness scaling factor must be chosen with care to effect the desired results.

Implementation—Frame process, Single image/pixel point process, Dual image/pixel point process The unsharp masking enhancement uses a group process to carry out the low pass filter operation. An appropriate low pass mask may be chosen. The low pass image is brightness scaled by a histogram shrink operation using a single image/pixel point process. The low pass image is then subtracted from the original, using a dual image/pixel point process. The resulting image may then be contrast enhanced by once again using a histogram stretch operation. This process is outlined:

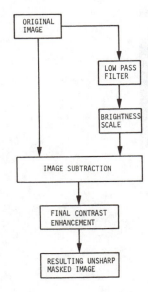

Figure IOS9-2 Unsharp masking operation flow diagram.

Results

Figure IOS9-3
(a) Original image displaying slight haze.

(b) Low passed image.

(c) Result of subtracting scaled low passed image from original, creating the final unsharp masked image.

Image Operation Study # 10

Operation—Shift and Difference Edge Enhancement

Description—The shift and difference operation provides the simplest means for generating edge enhancement in an image. Three edge enhancement options are available— vertical, horizontal, and the combination of the two. Vertical edge enhancement is accomplished by shifting the original image, pixel by pixel, to the left by one pixel. The shifted image is then subtracted from the original. This produces the brightness difference, or slope, of the two pixels. Whenever horizontally adjacent pixels were nearly the same brightness value in the original image, the output image will be dark. At a vertical edge, however, a large difference exists and will appear bright in the output image. The result is an image where vertical edges composed of black-to-white transitions in the left-to-right direction will appear bright. Constant or slowly changing brightness regions will appear dark.

Horizontal edge enhancement is formed by shifting the original image up by one pixel and carrying out the subtraction. Simultaneous vertical and horizontal enhancement requires a one-pixel shift left and up prior to the subtraction.

Application—The shift and difference enhancement is useful in the general extraction of vertical or horizontal edges. This enhancement can be of help in the analysis of an image having poor edge detail.

The output image of this enhancement takes on the appearance of a relief map of the original image. By adding a brightness scaled amount of the result back to the original, a uniquely highlighted image is produced.

Cautions—Because this operation subtracts one image from another, there is always the possibility of subtracting a bright level from a dark level. The result is an arithmetic underflow condition, which is usually handled by forcing the result to black. The net effect in a horizontal edge enhancement is the highlighting of edges composed of black-to-white transitions in the left-to-right direction. A white-to-black transition will not be enhanced because the arithmetic underflow of subtracting white from black will produce black as a result. Likewise, vertical edge enhancement will highlight black-to-white transitions in the top to bottom direction.

Implementation—Group process The most straightforward method in which to carry out this process is by actually shifting the original image and subtracting it from the original. However, the shifting process is often more difficult for an image processing system to handle than it may seem. The alternative method is done by way of a group process. The center coefficient is set to 1 and another coefficient to −1. The rest are left at zero. The overall effect is

149

the subtraction of a shifted image from its original. The mask coefficients always add to 0.

The three masks are given:

$$
\begin{matrix} 0 & 0 & 0 \\ -1 & 1 & 0 \\ 0 & 0 & 0 \end{matrix}
\qquad
\begin{matrix} 0 & -1 & 0 \\ 0 & 1 & 0 \\ 0 & 0 & 0 \end{matrix}
\qquad
\begin{matrix} -1 & 0 & 0 \\ 0 & 1 & 0 \\ 0 & 0 & 0 \end{matrix}
$$

Vertical edge enhancement

Horizontal edge enhancement

Vertical and horizontal edge enhancement

Results

Figure IOS10-1
(a) Original pattern image.

(b) Vertical shift and difference edge enhancement.

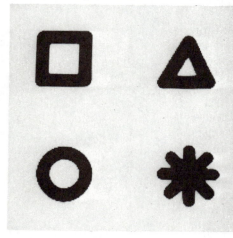

(c) Horizontal.

(d) Vertical and horizontal.

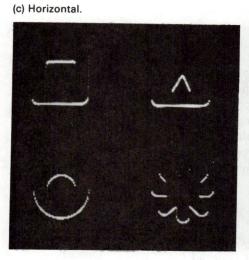

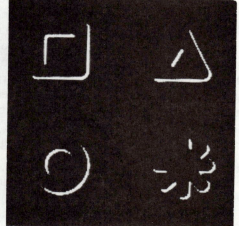

Figure IOS 10-2
(a) Original image of building.

(b) Vertical shift and difference edge enhancement.

(c) Horizontal.

(d) Vertical and horizontal.

Image Operation Study # 11

Operation—Gradient-Directional Edge Enhancement

Description—The gradient filter produces an output image where high spatial frequency components, such as edges, are highly accentuated. Low-frequency spatial components are attenuated sharply. The gradient enhancement is directional. It may be selected to occur in any one of the eight compass directions—N, NE, E, SE, S, SW, W, or NW. Edges composed of black-to-white transitions, in the defined direction, are enhanced to white. The level of white is dependent upon the amount of brightness change encountered in the original image. Constant brightness regions become black in the output image. The end result is a black background with white outlines of the objects in the original image.

Application—The gradient enhancement is useful in the extraction of object edges when the direction of the edges is of importance. This is often helpful in the analysis of images. By independently generating eight gradient images, an original image is broken into spatial directional parts. A host computer may then make judgements about object edge boundary directions within the image. Additionally, complex images may conceal object directional information that becomes evident once processed by the gradient operation. Such an application is in aerial geological surveys.

Cautions—The gradient operation produces a visual abstract of the original image. The process enhances edge information in a defined direction and, therefore, does not always bear a great resemblance to the original. The extracted information is used either in the enhancement of the original or in some image-analysis operation. As in other group processes, the 3 × 3 kernel size poses some restrictions. For the gradient operation, one limitation is that only eight directions of enhancement are available. Also, the angular width of enhancement for any selected direction is rather wide. Most applications have no trouble working within these limitations. If needed, though, a larger kernel size will provide additional flexibility.

Implementation—Group process The mask coefficients always add to 0. The eight directional masks are given.

```
  1  1  1        1  1  1       -1  1  1      -1 -1  1
  1 -2  1       -1 -2  1       -1 -2  1      -1 -2  1
 -1 -1 -1       -1 -1  1       -1  1  1       1  1  1
     N             NE             E             SE


 -1 -1 -1        1 -1 -1        1  1 -1       1  1  1
  1 -2  1        1 -2 -1        1 -2 -1       1 -2 -1
  1  1  1        1  1  1        1  1 -1       1 -1 -1
     S             SW             W             NW
```

Results

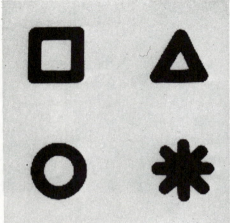

Figure IOS11-1
(a) Original pattern image.

(b) North direction gradient edge enhancement.

(c) Northeast.

(d) East.

(e) Southeast.

(f) South.

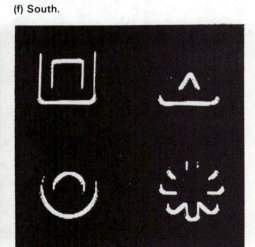

(g) Southwest.

(h) West.

(i) Northwest.

Figure IOS11-2
(a) Original image of building.

(b) North direction gradient edge enhancement.

(c) Northeast.

(d) East.

(e) Southeast.

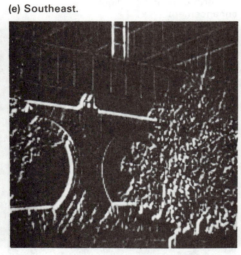

(f) South.

(g) Southwest.

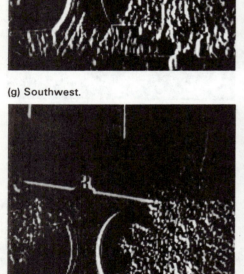

(h) West.

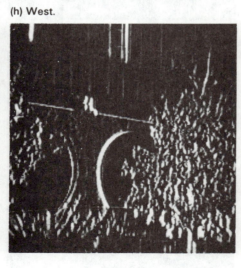

(i) Northwest.

Image Operation Study # 12

Operation—Laplacian Edge Enhancement

Description—The Laplacian edge enhancement produces an output image where high spatial frequency components such as edges are highly accentuated. Low spatial frequency components are attenuated sharply. The enhancement is omnidirectional. Edges composed of black-to-white transitions, in any direction, are enhanced to white. The level of white is dependent on the amount of brightness change encountered in the original image. Constant and linearly increasing or decreasing brightness regions become black in the output image. The end result is a black background with white outlines of the objects in the original image.

Application—The Laplacian filter is used in the extraction of object edges, or boundaries. Pattern recognition algorithms for use in robotics control often begin processing with a Laplacian operation.

For general sharpening of a poor image, good results are often obtained by adding a portion of the Laplacian of an image back to its original. The result is a highlighting of object boundaries within the image.

Figure IOS 12-1
(a) Original pattern image.

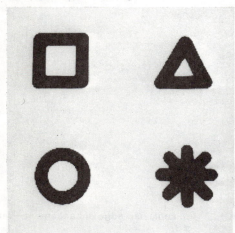

(b) Laplacian edge enhancement—mask #1.

(c) Laplacian edge enhancement—mask #2.

(d) Laplacian edge enhancement—mask #3.

Cautions—The Laplacian operation produces a visual abstract of the original image. The process enhances edge information and, therefore, does not always bear a great resemblance to the original. The extracted edge information may then be used in either the enhancement of the original or in some image analysis operation. As in other group processes, the 3×3 kernel size poses some restrictions on the frequency selectivity of the filter. By tailoring the mask coefficients and viewing the results, a suitable filter may be obtained.

Implementation—Group process The mask coefficients always add to 0. A large coefficient will generally appear in the center of the mask surrounded by smaller positive and negative coefficients. Three typical masks are given.

$$\begin{array}{ccc} -1 & -1 & -1 \\ -1 & 8 & -1 \\ -1 & -1 & -1 \end{array} \qquad \begin{array}{ccc} 0 & -1 & 0 \\ -1 & 4 & -1 \\ 0 & -1 & 0 \end{array} \qquad \begin{array}{ccc} 1 & -2 & 1 \\ -2 & 4 & -2 \\ 1 & -2 & 1 \end{array}$$

Mask 1   Mask 2   Mask 3

Figure IOS 12-2
(a) Original image of building.

(b) Laplacian edge enhancement—mask #1.

(c) Laplacian edge enhancement—mask #2.

(d) Laplacian edge enhancement—mask #3.

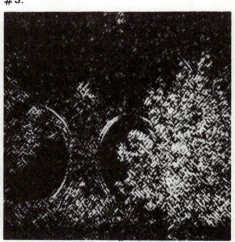

Image Operation Study # 13

Operation—Line Segment Enhancement

Description—Line segment enhancement produces an output image similar to edge enhancement operations. The change is that in addition to directional edge enhancement, the highlighted edge segments are produced in a more connected manner. The output image is a line segment enhancement in one of four directions—vertical, horizontal, left-to-right diagonal, or right-to-left diagonal.

In vertical line segment enhancement, two slopes are calculated for each row in the 3×3 kernel. The left neighboring pixel is subtracted from the center pixel, as is the right neighboring pixel. These two slopes are then subtracted from one another forming a slope-difference. Applied to the three rows of pixels in the 3×3 kernel, the sum of these operations yield the final result of the output pixel.

In the vertical enhancement, the net result is an image where all vertical edges appear bright and connected. Constant or slowly changing brightness regions appear dark. Horizontal and diagonal line segment enhancements are formed by changing the orientation of the group process mask.

Application—Line segment enhancements are useful in the extraction of edge information when it is desired to have edge segments as connected as possible. Where other edge enhancements tend to leave highlighted edges in a broken form, this enhancement attempts to connect severed segments. Additional passes of this enhancement will further connect broken segments. Ultimately, this type of operation acts as a good prelude to automatic machine inspection of parts where dimensions are to be measured from edge to edge.

Cautions—This enhancement process may generally be implemented without regard to downfalls. The final applicability to a particular application may be made by visual comparison with other processes.

Implementation—Group process The mask coefficients always add to 0. The four directional masks are given.

```
 −1   2 −1          −1 −1 −1
 −1   2 −1           2   2   2
 −1   2 −1          −1 −1 −1
```

Vertical line   **Horizontal line**
segment   **segment**
enhancement   **enhancement**

```
 −1 −1   2           2 −1 −1
 −1   2 −1          −1   2 −1
  2 −1 −1          −1 −1   2
```

Left-to-right   **Right-to-left**
diagonal   **diagonal**
line segment   **line segment**
enhancement   **enhancement**

Results

Figure IOS13-1
(a) Original pattern image. (b) Vertical line segment enhancement.

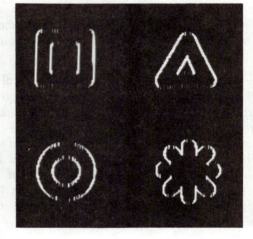

(c) Horizontal.

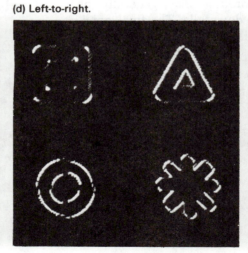

(d) Left-to-right.

(e) Right-to-left.

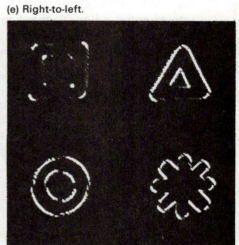

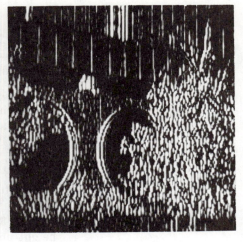

Figure IOS 13-2
(a) Original image of building.

(b) Vertical line segment enhancement.

(c) Horizontal.

(d) Left-to-right.

(e) Right-to-left.

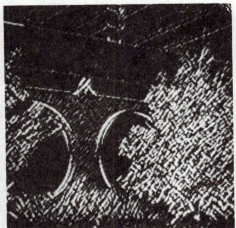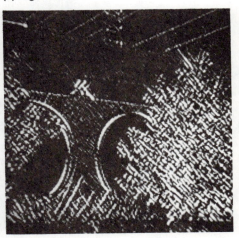

Image Operation Study #14

Operation—Image Scaling

Description—Image scaling allows the spatial enlargement and reduction of image size. A scaling factor, S, is selected. For an $S = 1$ the output image is identical to the original. An S less than 1 represents an image size reduction, whereas an S greater than 1 calls for an enlargement. In all cases, S is the scaling factor to occur in both horizontal and vertical directions.

To produce an image reduced in size by a factor of 3, $S = 1/3$ is selected. The output image will be 1/3 the height and 1/3 the width of the original. The reduction is accomplished by eliminating two out of every three pixels in both the horizontal and vertical directions.

In producing an image enlarged by a factor of 3, $S = 3$ is selected. Since the output image must be contained by the same frame size as the original, the final enlargement will be a section of the original, blown up to occupy the entire frame. The enlargement is done by replicating every pixel 3 times in both the horizontal and vertical directions.

Application—Image scaling is used in the geometric manipulation of images prior to or following various processing operations. In particular, dual image/pixel point processes often require that the two input images be in tight geometric alignment prior to their combination. Improper alignment can produce undesired fringe effects around object boundaries.

Enlarging a portion of an image can help in the visual analysis of detailed objects. Furthermore, an enlargement may allow visible recognition of an image's degradation, helping in the selection of corrective processing.

In graphic arts, image reduction facilitates the combination of various input images into a composite image.

Cautions—Image reduction is carried out by eliminating pixels, which compresses the spatial dimensions of the frame. As a result, spatial resolution is reduced. Once an image has been reduced, the stripped pixels are lost and may not be recovered except by retrieving the original image from some master storage source. In enlargement, pixels of a selected area are replicated to stretch the spatial dimensions of a portion of the image to the full frame size. Hence, no image data is lost from the enlarged region. The remainder of the original image, though, is entirely lost. Again, recovering the lost image data requires retrieving the original from a master source.

Implementation—Frame process This operation is generally carried out in software by a host computer. The basic flow chart is given, where

S = scaling factor
x = input image pixel address
y = input image line address
x' = output image pixel address
y' = output image line address
PRC = pixel replication counter
LRC = line replication counter

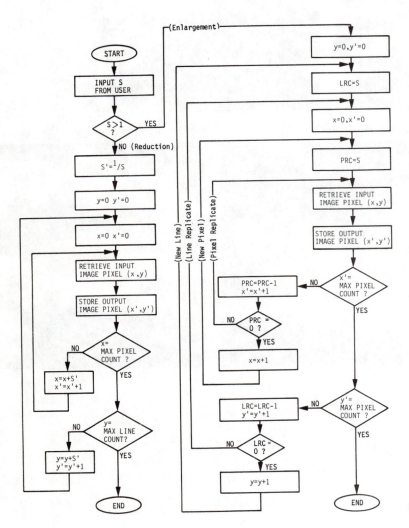

Figure IOS 14-1 Image scaling flow diagram.

Results

Figure IOS14-2

(a) Original image.

(b) Various spatial image size reductions.

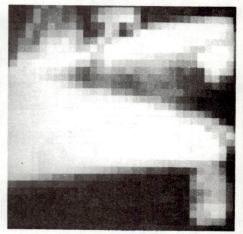

(c) Times 2 enlargement.

(d) Times 4 enlargement.

(e) Times 6 enlargement.

Image Operation Study # 15

Operation—Image Rotation

Description—Image rotation allows spatial rotation of an input image. The angle of rotation, θ, is selected. The rotation algorithm produces an output image geometrically rotated counterclockwise through the angle θ. The rotation occurs about the image center point. The pixel coordinate origin is defined as (0,0) at the center of the image. Hence, for a 256 $\times$ 256 image, pixel coordinates range from -127 to 128, left to right, and the line coordinates range from -127 to 128, top to bottom.

Application—Image rotation is used in the geometric manipulation of images prior to or following various processing operations. Often dual image/pixel point processes use rotations to bring the two input images into spatial registration prior to operating upon them.

In graphic arts, image rotation facilitates the combination of various input images into a composite output image.

Cautions—In rotating an image composed of fixed discrete pixels, the input pixels will typically not transform directly into output pixel locations (except when θ is a multiple of 90°). Because of this, interpolation algorithms are often

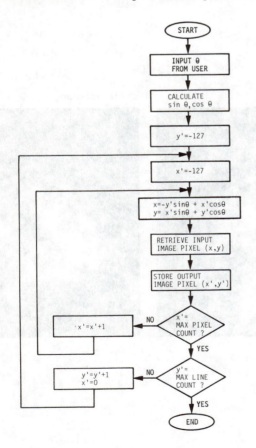

Figure IOS15-1 Image rotation flow diagram (rotation about image frame center point).

employed. These algorithms break a transformed input pixel's brightness into four parts, each contributing to one of the four output pixels surrounding the calculated output image pixel location. Interpolation schemes take on a variety of forms—some rough approximations, some more exact. The tradeoff is often related to required processing time. Depending on the amount of detail present in an image along with the final requirements of the image, an appropriate interpolation scheme may be employed.

Implementation—Frame process This operation is generally carried out in software by a host computer. The basic flow chart is given, where

θ = angle of counterclockwise rotation
x = input image pixel address
y = input image line address
x' = output image pixel address
y' = output image line address

It should be noted that this algorithm uses reverse pixel mapping. Input pixel coordinates are calculated for each and every possible output coordinate. Due to the non-one-to-one pixel transformation of the rotation operation, this scheme insures that all output pixels will acquire a new rotated value.

Results

Figure IOS15-2

(a) Original image.

(b) 330° rotation.

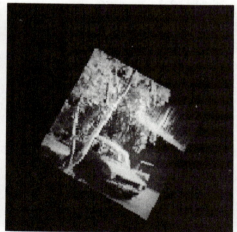

(c) 60° rotation.

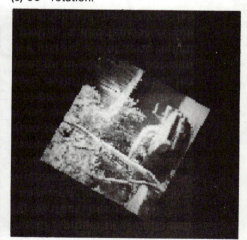

Image Operation Study #16

Operation—Image Translation

Description—Image translation allows the side to side, up and down spatial movement of an image. The translation offset values, T_x and T_y are specified. T_x is the number of pixels, positive or negative, that the image is to be shifted in the horizontal direction. T_y represents the number of pixels that the image is to be shifted vertically. The output image is identical to the original except spatially shifted horizontally and vertically.

Application—Image translation is used in the geometric manipulation of images prior to or following various processing operations. Often dual image/pixel point processes use translations to bring the two input images into spatial registration prior to operating upon them.

In graphic arts, image translation facilitates the combination of various input images into a composite output image.

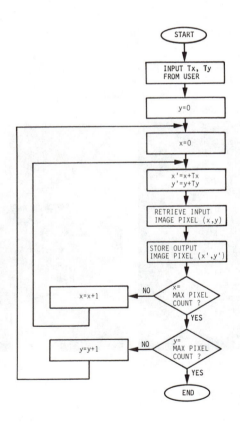

Figure IOS16-1 Image translation flow diagram.

165

Cautions—Loss of image data cannot result from a translation operation. Wraparound effects are prevalent, though. Normally, a reduced image is translated from one area of the frame to another. When the image is full size, or large with respect to the amount of translation, often a side will translate off the image frame. The pixels that go off one side come up on the adjacent side of the frame. The image may be thought of as on a special loop that may roll up and down or side to side. The image will roll off one side and wrap around to the other.

Implementation—**Frame process** This operation is generally carried out in software by a host computer. The basic flow chart is given, where

$T_x=$ horizontal translation
$T_y=$ vertical translation
$x =$ input image pixel address
$y =$ input image line address
$x'=$ output image pixel address
$y'=$ output image line address

Results

Figure IOS 16-2
(a) Original image.

(b) Various spatial image translations.

(c) Wraparound effect on a large format image.

Image Operation Study # 17

Operation—Image Averaging

Description—The image averaging operation produces an output image that is the average of two input images. Images are combined on a pixel-by-pixel basis. Each pixel brightness in the first image is averaged, with its corresponding pixel brightness in the second image. When applying this operation to two completely different image scenes, the result is a composite image of both. If the scenes are identical, the resultant image will be similar, with a decrease in any present random noise.

Application—The predominant use of this operation is in image noise reduction. Random "snow" noise present in an image changes spatial position from frame to frame. Providing that more than one frame of the same scene is available, reduction of this type of noise is possible. Averaging two or more of the images diminishes the presence of the "snow" because the noise becomes averaged with good pixel data. If enough frames are averaged together, the net result will be an image visually devoid of the noise.

Averaging two images of totally different scenes produces a result where both scenes appear superimposed upon one another. This effect is found useful in some applications.

Cautions—This operation may generally be implemented without regard to downfalls.

Implementation—Dual image/pixel point process The image averaging operation uses a dual image/pixel point process to carry out the pixel-by-pixel addition. In the addition of two 8-bit pixels, a 9-bit result is produced. This result is then brightness scaled by a factor of two, to a valid 8-bit pixel value, by the dual image/pixel point processor output map, M. The equation for this operation is given.

$$O(x,y) = M[I_1(x,y) + I_2(x,y)]$$

Figure IOS17-1 Brightness scale divide by 2 map.

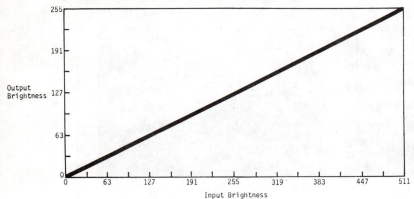

Output Brightness

Input Brightness

167

Results

Figure IOS17-2

(a) Original image #1.

(b) Original image #2.

(c) Average of #1 and #2.

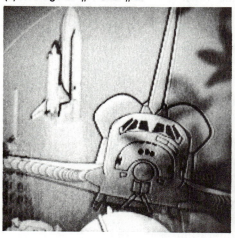

(d) Original image corrupted by noise.

(e) Second original image corrupted by noise.

(f) Averaged image pair with reduced noise content.

Image Operation Study #18

Operation—Image Subtraction: Motion Detection, Background Subtraction

Description—Image subtraction is accomplished by taking the pixel-by-pixel difference of two input images. This process is normally applied to similar images of basically the same scene. The resulting output image is predominantly black where elements of the scene are identical in the two images. Objects that are not present in one image or have changed spatial locations show up upon the black background.

Application—Two predominant uses for image subtraction are motion detection and background subtraction operations. In motion detection, two images of the same scene are used. Identical portions of the images will subtract out to black in the output image. Differences in the two images, such as objects that have moved, will show up clearly in both locations of the output image. Hence, motion and direction are made evident. If the time between image acquisition is known, then speed of the moved object may also be calculated. One particular application of motion detection is in medical blood flow analysis.

Background subtraction is an identical operation to motion detection; however, it is thought of in different terms. Complicated scenes with a lot of detail may make it difficult to detect subtle changes from frame to frame. Here, the idea is to subtract out common background image information, leaving only differences for analysis. Subtraction of two images, one of only the background, allows the differences to be made immediately detectable. Medical X-ray imagery often uses this type of operation. Complicated surrounds in an image are eliminated by taking an image prior to the patient's ingestion of a radio-opaque liquid. A second image is then taken once the areas of interest have been highlighted by the liquid. When the first image is subtracted from the second, only the highlighted features are left. The complexity of analysis is greatly reduced when working with an image enhanced through this process.

Cautions—This operation may generally be implemented without regard to downfalls.

Implementation—Dual image/pixel point process Image subtraction uses a dual image/pixel point process to carry out the pixel-by-pixel subtraction. In the subtraction of the two 8-bit pixels, a 9-bit result is produced. The ninth bit represents a borrow, or arithmetic underflow. To faithfully reproduce all differences in pixel brightness, an absolute value map is used to insure that all results are positive, and 8-bit. This function is handled by the dual image/pixel point processor output map, M. The equation for this operation is given.

$$O(x,y) = M[I_1(x,y) - I_2(x,y)]$$

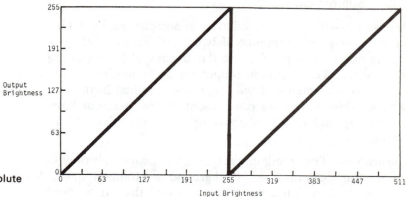

Figure IOS 18-1 Brightness scale absolute value map.

Results

Figure IOS 18-2

(a) Original image with foreground and background.

(b) Image of only background.

(c) Image subtraction yielding only foreground object.

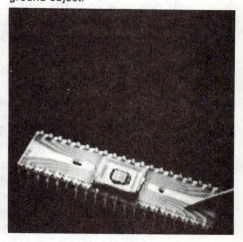

(d) Original image of printed circuit board with components properly placed.

(e) Board with intergrated circuit improperly placed.

(f) Subtraction yielding only placement discrepancy with background detail removed.

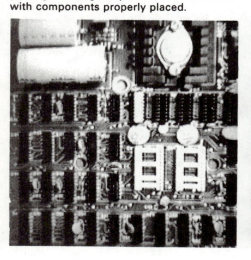

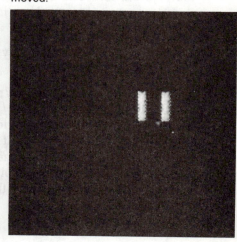

Image Operation Study # 19

Operation—Logical Image Combination: AND, OR, EXclusive-OR

Description—This operation provides for the logical pixel-by-pixel combination of two input images. Such operations between images include AND, OR and EXclusive-OR functions. An output pixel value is calculated by logically combining the two respective input pixels in a bit-by-bit fashion.

Application—The AND and OR image combinations are normally used to mask and add together images. We use the AND function to mask off portions of an image. Given an image of which we wish to retain only a small section, a second image may be generated to be a mask. The mask image is composed of pixels having a binary value equal to all 0s (black), where the original image should be masked, or 1s (white) where it should be allowed to appear in the output image. The AND combination of the two images produces the final masked image.

Image OR combinations are used to add together subimages into a composite output image. Given that two subimages do not spatially overlap and are masked, they may be ORed together combining both into a single output image.

The EXclusive-OR combination may sometimes be found useful as a simple image comparing operation. Pixels are combined bit by bit, producing an output image displaying black where the two input pixels are *exactly* identical. Where the two pixels are not perfectly identical, the output pixel will be something other than black, depending on the actual bit-for-bit comparison.

Cautions—Performing the AND or OR combinations on images that have pixels other than black or white in overlapping regions often will produce strange results. This is because the operations happen on a bit-by-bit fashion. The result of an AND or OR of two pixel brightnesses does not really hold any practical significance. In the case of EXclusive-ORing two images, if two respective input pixels are not exactly identical, the resulting value means very little. The significance is found in resulting pixels that are totally black, for these pixels are identical in the two input images.

Implementation—Dual image/pixel point process All logical image combinations are carried out by the image/pixel point processor.

Results

Figure IOS19-1
(a) Original image.

(b) Mask image.

(c) AND combination of original and mask images yielding a masked version of the original.

(d) Subimage of road map.

(e) OR combination of subimage and masked original image.

(f) Gray level image where all pixel brightnesses equal 64.

(g) EXclusive-OR combination of original with gray level images, yielding image with white pixels wherever the original image pixels equal 64.

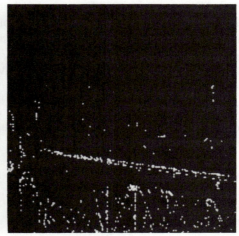

172

Further Reading & References

I. **College-level texts on digital image processing (requiring some knowledge of higher mathematics)**

1. H.C. ANDREWS, Computer Techniques in Image Processing, Academic Press, New York, 1970.

2. H.C. ANDREWS, B.R. HUNT, Digital Image Restoration, Prentice-Hall, Englewood Cliffs, New Jersey, 1977.

3. K.R. CASTLEMAN, Digital Image Processing, Prentice-Hall, Englewood Cliffs, New Jersey, 1979.

4. R.C. GONZALEZ, P. WINTZ, Digital Image Processing, Addison-Wesley, Reading, Massachusetts, 1977.

5. A. ROSENFELD, Picture Processing by Computer, Academic Press, New York, 1969.

6. A. ROSENFELD, A.C. KAK, Digital Picture Processing, Academic Press, New York, 1976.

7. A. ROSENFELD, A.C. KAK, Digital Picture Processing, 2ed, Vol. 1 and 2, Academic Press, New York, 1982.

8. W.K. PRATT, Digital Image Processing, John Wiley, New York, 1978.

II. **Practical-level texts on digital image processing (relying on a more intuitive rather than rigorous approach)**

1. W.B. GREEN, Digital Image Processing—A Systems Approach, Van Nostrand Reinhold, New York, 1983.

2. A. ROSENFELD, Digital Picture Analysis, Springer-Verlag, Berlin Heidelberg, 1976.

III. **Selected papers dealing with digital image processing and associated topics**

1. H.C. ANDREWS, Tutorial and Selected Papers in Digital Image Processing (collection of papers), IEEE Computer Society, New York, 1978.

2. R. BERNSTEIN, Digital Image Processing for Remote Sensing, (collection of papers), IEEE Press, 1978.

3. J.K. AGGARWAL, R.O. DUDA, A. ROSENFELD, Computer Methods in Image Analysis, (collection of papers) IEEE Press, 1977.

4. F.C. BILLINGSLEY, Digital Image Processing for Information Extraction, Institute of Physics, Conference Series No. 13: Machine Perception of Patterns and Pictures, 1972.

5. W.B. GREEN, Computer Image Processing—The Viking Experience, IEEE Transactions and Consumer Electronics, Vol. CE-23, IEEE, New York, August 1977.

6. H.C. ANDREWS, Digital Image Processing, IEEE Spectrum, IEEE, New York, April 1979.

7. F. W. CAMPBELL, The Human Eye as an Optical Filter, Proceedings of the IEEE, Vol. 56, No. 6, IEEE, New York, June 1968.

8. F.W. CAMPBELL, Contrast and Spatial Frequency, Scientific American, New York, November 1974.

IV. **College-level texts on general digital signal processing (requiring some knowledge of higher mathematics)**

1. A.V. OPPENHEIM, Applications of Digital Signal Processing, Prentice-Hall, Englewood Cliffs, New Jersey, 1978.

2. A.V. OPPENHEIM, R.W. SCHAFER, Digital Signal Processing, Prentice-Hall, Englewood Cliffs, New Jersey, 1975.

3. L.R. RABINER, B. GOLD, Theory and Application of Digital Signal Processing, Prentice-Hall, Englewood Cliffs, New Jersey, 1975.

V. **Texts dealing with the related fields of digital image processing**

1. CONRAC DIVISION, CONRAC CORP., Raster Graphics Handbook, California, 1980.

2. W.M. NEWMAN, R.F. SPROULL, Principles of Interactive Computer Graphics, McGraw-Hill, New York, 1979.

Glossary

(Terms listed as follows are defined as used in the context of digital image processing)

Active line time—The portion of a video signal where visual information lies. Nonactive times are composed of sync and blanking periods.

Aliasing—The phenomenon where the spatial frequency of a sampled signal is not preserved due to undersampling at a rate less than two times the original frequency content.

Amplitude—The voltage level, representing a brightness, of a video signal at any given point in time.

Analog to Digital converter (A/D)—An element of image acquisition that serves to convert an analog video voltage level sample, or pixel, to a binary quantity.

Arithmetic Logic Unit (ALU)—An element in the image processor hardware allowing the arithmetic and logical combination of pixel brightness quantities.

Aspect ratio—The proportion of an image size given in terms of the horizontal length versus the vertical height. An aspect ratio of 4:3 means the horizontal dimension of the image frame is 4/3 the vertical dimension.

Bit—The fundamental digital quantity representing either the true (1) or false (0) condition.

Blanking—The suppression of video information during

sync and image border periods, forcing the display monitor to display black.

Brightness—The value associated with a pixel representing its gray value from black to white.

Brightness resolution—The accuracy at which the brightness of a pixel is measured, or quantized. For instance, a resolution of four bits represents 16 possible gray values.

Byte—A binary quantity of eight bits.

Combination function—The operation that defines how two or more images are mixed to form a new resultant image.

Continuous tone—A term describing a photographic print where brightnesses appear consistent and uninterrupted.

Contouring—An effect present in an image as a result of low brightness resolution appearing as bands of sharp brightness change.

Contrast—A measure of brightness content in an image. High contrast implies mainly dark black and bright white content; medium contrast implies a good spread from black to white; low contrast implies a small spread of gray values.

Contrast enhancement—Any operation serving to increase or decrease the contrast attributes of an image in order to bring out definition not clearly visible in the original.

Control points—Spatial pixel locations defined in a rubber sheet transformation, representing a geometric contortion to be evoked. Surrounding pixels follow in the transformation through spatial interpolation methods.

Convolution—The mathematical operation whereby group processes are implemented.

Convolution coefficient—A numeric value defining the weight that a pixel within a convolution kernel takes on in a group process.

Convolution kernel—The size of the pixel array used in the calculation of an output pixel in a group process.

Convolution mask—The array of convolution coefficients defining a group process.

Data bandwidth—The amount of data, defined in bits, transferred in a single cycle to and from the image store memory.

Data compression—An operation that, through various techniques, reduces the data content needed to represent an image.

Degrees of freedom—The flexibility afforded in the definition of an operation; generally associated with the kernel size in a group process.

Differential pulse code modulation (DPCM)—An image data compression technique relying on the coding of adjacent pixel brightness differences rather than their absolute brightnesses.

Digital image—An image composed of discrete pixels of digitally quantized brightnesses.

Digital to analog converter (D/A)—An element of an image display system that serves to convert a binary quantity sample, or pixel, to an analog video voltage level for display.

Digitization—The act of sampling and quantizing an analog video signal.

Display—The means by which an image is viewed. A television monitor is a typical display device.

Dynamic RAM—A random access memory device offering high data storage density and low power, but requiring refreshing in order to maintain data storage integrity.

Dynamic range—The spread of gray values found in a given image. High dynamic range implies a wide spread of gray values whereas low dynamic range indicates a small spread and, therefore, low contrast.

Edge enhancement—Any operation that accentuates edge details within an image. Such operations include the shift and difference, gradient, and Laplacian enhancements.

External access memory cycle—The access cycle to and from the two-port image store memory in which image data is retrieved and stored for processing.

Field—The set of either the even or odd lines in an image. The idea of a field is used when dealing with an interlaced video display as defined by the standard video format.

Frame process—In general, any image process. Subsets of frame processes include point and group processes.

Frame rate—The frequency at which an image is completely updated on the viewer display monitor.

Frequency transform—An operation that breaks down an image into its fundamental spatial frequency components for subsequent analysis or filtering.

Geometric manipulation—Any operation that alters the spatial geometry of an image. Examples include scaling, rotation, translation, and rubber sheet transformation.

Gradient edge enhancement—An edge enhancement operation possessing a directional quality. With a 3×3 kernel size, gradient operations may be evoked to enhance edges in any one of the eight compass directions.

Gray level—The brightness value assigned to a pixel. A value may range from black, through the grays, to white.

Gray scale—The brightnesses available as valid gray levels for a given image processing system. The gray scale represents the discrete gray levels defined in a system—for instance, an 8-bit system includes the values from 0 through 255.

Group process—An image process used to evoke spatial filtering operations. In performing a group process, resultant pixels are calculated as a weighted average of neighboring pixels surrounding the pixel being processed. A convolution kernel of 3×3 is typically used.

Histogram—The graphical representation of the gray-scale occupancy of an image. With the horizontal axis representing gray level and the vertical axis representing number of pixels, the histogram presents an easy-to-read indication of image contrast and brightness dynamic range.

Histogram slide—The addition or subtraction of a constant brightness to all pixels within an image. This operation facilitates contrast and brightness enhancements, with the end effect of sliding gray values up or down the scale.

Histogram stretch—The multiplication or division of all pixels within an image by a constant value. This operation facilitates contrast and brightness enhancement, with the end effect of stretching or shrinking gray scale occupancy.

High pass filter—An image operation that enhances high spatial frequencies or attenuates low frequencies in an image. This operation is used to bring out details difficult to see in the original.

Horizontal sync—The portion of a video signal indicating the end of a line of video information. This sync pulse is used by video equipment in order to maintain line synchronization with the incoming video signal.

Image analysis—Any image operation intended to numerically tabulate some aspect of an image.

Image coding—Any image operation used to reduce the amount of data required to describe the content of an image.

Image operation—Any algorithm for evoking a quality enhancement, analysis, or coding upon an image.

Image process—Any method for implementing an image operation. Such processes include point, group, and frame processes.

Image quality enhancement—Any image operation serving to bring out some aspect not visible in the original.

Image store—The memory array within an image processing system that stores an image for subsequent display and processing.

Intensity—The radiated light energy associated with an image scene or portion thereof.

Interlace—The technique used in the standard video format where the field of odd image lines is displayed followed by the field of even lines. Interlacing is used to reduce noticeable flickering in an image display.

Interpolation—The mathematical technique used with geometric operations when the output pixel coordinates do not land exactly on a defined pixel grid point. Interpolation divides the transformed pixel's brightness and distributes portions to the four surrounding valid pixel locations.

Laplacian edge enhancement—An edge enhancement operation possessing an omnidirectional quality. Laplacian operations accentuate all edge details within an image, regardless of spatial orientation.

Line—The coordinate used for defining the vertical spatial location of a pixel within an image.

Line segment enhancement—Any image operation that accentuates line segment details within an image. With a 3 × 3 kernel size, line segments in either the vertical, horizontal, or either diagonal may be enhanced.

Look-up table (LUT)—The means for implementing a point process. The look-up table is a memory device loaded with the map values for a given point process. Input pixel values act as the address to the memory, with the output, or map value, subsequently being generated as the data at the addressed location.

Low pass filter—Any operation that enhances low spatial frequencies or attenuates high frequencies in an image. This operation is used to bring out elements of an image difficult to see in the original.

Mach-band effect—A visual illusion created by the photosite interactions and response characteristics of the eye. The effect is a perceived edge accentuation when viewing sharp black to white transitions.

Map—A graphical representation of the mapping function used in a point process. The map graphically defines how input pixel brightnesses are transformed to resultant output brightnesses.

Mapping function—The mathematical equation defining a point process. The mapping function is the formula that calculates resultant output pixel brightnesses from input brightnesses.

Memory cycle—Any one of a variety of sequences used to access data in or out of a memory device such as the image store.

Memory cycle time—The time necessary to complete a single data access to a memory device such as the image store.

Median filter—An image spatial filtering operation based on an input pixel and its eight neighbors. The resultant value is the median of the nine pixel brightnesses such that an equal number of values are greater than and less than the resulting median output value.

Monochrome—A term pertaining to an image represented by a single color. Generally, a monochrome image is presented as black and white.

Non-square pixel—A pixel with spatial dimensions other than 1 by 1. For instance, an image with an aspect ratio of 4:3 yields non-square pixels with the dimensions of 4 to 3.

Nyquist criterion—The theoretical requirement used to define sampling rate in an image acquisition system. The sampling rate must be twice that of the highest spatial frequency to be resolved in the reconstructed image.

Phased memory access—A memory timing scheme accessing individual memory banks at different times, eliminating the need for large pixel data buffers but requiring complex sequencing circuitry.

Photometric correction—An image operation that corrects image sensor response and geometric irregularities.

Pixel—The fundamental picture element of a digital image. Also, the coordinate used for defining the horizontal spatial location of a pixel within an image.

Point process—An image process used to evoke contrast and brightness alterations upon an image. An input pixel brightness is transformed through a mapping function creating the resultant output pixel brightness value.

Quantization—The act of converting an analog pixel brightness to a digital quantity.

Random access memory (RAM)—A memory device with the qualities of allowing arbitrary reading or writing of a desired data location.

Reconstruction—The act of reformulating an analog video signal for display from digitally stored image data.

Resolution—The accuracy at which a parameter is divided into discrete levels. Pertinent resolutions in an image processing system are those of brightness, spatial, and frame rate.

RGB—Notation when dealing with an image acquisition or display system handling color images composed of Red, Green, and Blue components.

Rotation—A geometric image operation used to rotate an image through an angle θ.

Rubber sheet transformation—A geometric image operation used to contort an image through the use of specified control points.

Run-length coding—An image data compression technique relying on the coding of strings of pixels of identical brightness rather than absolute brightness.

Sample—A discrete pixel of analog brightness. A sample is subsequently quantized, yielding a pixel of digital brightness.

Sampling—The chopping of the analog video signal into discrete pixels but not including the quantization process.

Scaling—A geometric image operation used to enlarge or shrink an image.

Shift-and-difference edge enhancement—An edge enhancement operation known for its simplistic implementation. An image is skewed by one pixel either up or to the left and then subtracted from the original generating horizontal or vertical edge enhancements.

Simultaneous contrast—A visual illusion created by the photosite interactions and response characteristics of the eye. The effect is to make a region of an image appear brighter or darker depending upon the surrounding brightness.

Spatial—Pertaining to the two-dimensional nature of an image.

Spatial convolution—The mathematical operation whereby group processes are implemented.

Spatial filtering—The set of image operations allowing the attenuation or accentuation of spatial frequencies within an image. Such operations include low and high pass filtering and are generally carried out by a group process.

Spatial frequency—The concept dealing with the rate of brightness change in an image. Brightness fluctuations occurring in close proximity to one another represent high spatial frequencies, whereas regions of relatively constant brightness represent low spatial frequencies.

Spatial resolution—The accuracy at which an image is divided into discrete pixels. For instance an image of 256 line by 256 pixel spatial resolution represents a spatial resolution of 65,536 pixels in the frame.

Standard video format—The RS-170 timing and voltage level specification dictating the qualities of the United States black-and-white commercial television signal.

Static RAM—A random access memory device offering simple design requirements without the need of refreshing circuitry, but requiring higher power and having lower data storage density than dynamic RAM devices.

Sync—The portion of a video signal indicating either the end of a field or end of a line of video information.

Sync extraction—The electronic detection of sync pulses within a video signal for use in synchronizing video equipment with the incoming signal.

Translation—A geometric image operation used to move an image from one spatial location to another.

Two-port memory—A memory architecture giving two independent data access paths to a memory device. Used in image store design, this technique allows the time-shared access of video data and data to be processed in and out of the memory array.

Undersampling—The sampling of an analog video signal at a rate less than that required by the Nyquist Criterion to resolve a given spatial frequency.

Unsharp masking enhancement—An image operation used to produce a sharpened version of an image. By subtracting a brightness scaled, low passed image from its original yields the sharpened resultant image.

Vertical sync—The portion of a video signal indicating the end of a field of video information. This sync pulse is used by video equipment in order to maintain field synchronization with the incoming video signal.

Video—Pertaining to the electronic form of image transmission.

Video access cycle—The access cycle to and from the two-port image store memory in which image data is stored from an input device, such as a camera, and retrieved for display upon a viewer monitor.

Weighted average—The mathematical operation used in spatial convolution to compute the result of each output pixel based on an input pixel and its eight neighbors. Each pixel and its neighbors are multiplied by their respective convolution coefficients as defined in the convolution mask. The results are summed, yielding the weighted average.